D0884136

68350

QP
251
R62

WITHDRAWN

Rorvik

Your baby's sex: now you can
choose

Date Due

JA 2 0 '71	NOV 26 '75	MY 8 '87	
AG 1 3 7	FEB 2 9 '80	JUN 1 8 1990	
	JUN 1 2 '80	JUN 2 1 1990	
NO 21 72	OCT 7 '80	MAY 8 1991	
MAR 6 74	OCT 21 '80	JUL 11 1991	
DEC 30 74	MAY 22 '82	APR 2 4 '07	
OC 16 74	JUN 5 '82	MAY 3 1 2002	
DEC 10 74	JAN 27 83		
MAY 21 75	OCT 10 83		
NOV 13 75	OCT 19 83		
NOV 26 75	APR 16 86		

WITHDRAWN

Your Baby's Sex: Now You Can Choose

Your Baby's Sex:

Now You Can Choose

David M. Rorvik *with*
Landrum B. Shettles, M.D., Ph.D.

Dodd, Mead & Company • *New York*

Library of Congress Catalog Card Number: 75-114811

Printed in the United States of America

by The Cornwall Press, Inc.
Cornwall, N. Y.

This book is exuberantly dedicated to the overthrow of the so-called "50–50 Club," an invention of complacent baby doctors who *erroneously* tell their patients that as a "gift" of Nature they have a 50 percent chance of begetting offspring of the desired sex, and that beyond this, nothing can be done for them.

Contents

part II:
SEX IN THE FUTURE

Illustrations

Introduction

Despite the almost universal unconcern of baby doctors, few topics interest prospective parents more than the sex of their children. Since earliest times, records show, men have tried to choose the sex of their children, indulging in macabre rituals and superstition, even selling their souls to imaginary devils in efforts to beget a son or a daughter. Great kingdoms have been disrupted for the simple reason that a queen—or a whole series of them—could not produce a male heir. On a less exalted level, thousands of blameless wives have been cast out of their homes because they have similarly failed to give birth to children of the sex desired by their husbands.

Today, the anguish that can result from such "failures" is as great as it was in days of old—perhaps greater since we have come to expect so much of modern science and medicine. Parents are understandably exasperated by

doctors who can do no better than offer them member-
ship in the so-called "50–50 Club," about which we will
learn more as we go along. Parents have only to look at
the front page of their daily newspaper to see that this
is an age of scientific miracles. Atomic energy is being
harnessed for peaceful purposes, men have left their
footprints on the moon and are already talking of doing
the same on Mars in the next decade, hearts are being
transplanted all around the world, molecular biologists
are unlocking the deepest secrets of "inner space," and
medical researchers are already setting up their laboratories for test-tube babies. Why then, parents ask, is
such a seemingly simple—and important—matter as the
sex of one's children beyond the reach of science?

Fortunately, it no longer is, and that is what this
book is all about. Still, one wonders why it has taken
science so long to arrive at some of the conclusions and
discoveries that are discussed in the pages that follow.
The answer, in part, has to do with the traditional notion
that the control of life, including the sex of our children,
is the *sole* responsibility of the Creator. This notion has
often served as a camouflage for ignorance, a camouflage
behind which the medical profession itself has taken
refuge. In times past, if a doctor couldn't cure a disease,
he would simply write off the resulting death as "God's
will." In addition, for long periods of time, anatomists
and other researchers were denied access to the human
body for religious reasons. If they wanted to study the
construction and workings of the human body they had

to do so indirectly, through the study of animals that had little in common with man. In the Middle Ages, for example, no one was allowed to dissect a human corpse.

These taboos have continued right into the present age. Medical students, in fact, were unable to study directly the earliest stages of human development—when sperm and egg join to form a new individual—until fifteen years ago; at that time this microscopic drama was enacted outside the womb, and pictures of it became available for the first time ever. (As we shall see, it was the same doctor who is now at the forefront of research in sex selection who provided those historic pictures.) Why was it that medical students had to settle for a shadowy picture of human embryology—through observation of lab animals? Partly because of the age-old fear of "manipulating" life and partly because generations of scientists before them, similarly inhibited by their own prejudices and retarded by lack of proper equipment, had laid so little groundwork for meaningful research.

Fortunately, today both ignorance and prejudices are falling by the way, and human reproduction is finally coming under the full glare of the medical spotlight. Now all that must be overcome is an unwillingness to adapt to something new, an unwillingness to readjust. This book has a twofold purpose: 1) To let the baby doctor know about research in this field and thus, hopefully, facilitate that readjustment, and 2) to give the reader of this book the opportunity to use what knowledge is available in an effort to select the sex of his off-spring—in his own home and with a high expectation of success.

Before proceeding directly to the techniques of sex selection, based primarily on the findings of Dr. Landrum B. Shettles of the famed Columbia-Presbyterian Medical Center in New York City, we need some background in the history and dynamics of sex selection. Chapters One and Two are an effort to provide just that. In Chapter One, "Man Versus Mother Nature: Early Attempts at Sex Selection," those of you who think that your desire to choose the sex of your children is something new will find a few surprises. And you will see in the course of it, that even such great early philosophers and scientists as Socrates and Aristotle had what can only be described as some pretty weird ideas on how to select sex. Getting drunk or wearing boots to bed during the critical inter-course were two of the milder "solutions" to the problem.

In Chapter Two—"Science to the Rescue: The Saga of X and Y"—we explore the world of life-before-birth and, in fact, life-before-conception. Until recently this was a realm of deep mystery, an inaccessible world that had been misunderstood for ages. In this chapter we focus on the scientific rather than the superstitious, on fact rather than fantasy. The means by which Nature determines sex is revealed in simple language; we "see" in action both the egg and the sperm, acknowledging the complexities of the first and the power and agility of the second.

With the stage set for discovery, we come to Chapter Three: "Breakthrough: *Now* You Can Choose." In this chapter we see how some of the knowledge discussed in the previous chapter can be put to work to help you select the sex of your children. At the heart of all this is a discovery made by Dr. Shettles, leading to the scientific procedures he has developed, one designed to produce boys, the other, girls. This is the crucial chapter: it tells you not only how Dr. Shettles arrived at his conclusions but also details the ways in which you can profitably make use of them.

Chapter Four consists of excerpts from the hundreds of letters that poured in following publication of a brief magazine article about Dr. Shettles' work. Answers to the letter-writers' questions will, hopefully, personalize some of the data discussed in the previous chapter and clear up questions you may have in your own mind. This chapter shows how even the type of shorts a man wears can have an influence on the sex of his offspring. (This may *sound* crazy, but save your chuckles until you hear what an eminent Boston doctor has to say about it.)

In the final chapter of Part One a question is posed: "What If Everyone Wants Boys?" Here we examine the possible consequences of our new ability to choose sex. Might it result in a world top-heavy with boys or brimming over with girls? If one sex predominates, could this lead to increased homosexuality and other problems? Could it, as one sociologist has seriously suggested, result in the downfall of the two-party political system in the

United States? Looking at the other side of the coin, in what ways—beyond making for better-balanced families—might the ability to choose sex benefit society? All of these questions will be taken up in Chapter Five.

Part Two, "Sex in the Future," examines the so-called biological revolution and some of the things it has in store for us in terms of the selection and control of sex. In the first of this section's two chapters, we consider some possible means of selecting sex in the future, most of which will sound a little like science fiction. Some of these procedures, however, are already under development and, according to some prominent scientists, may be applied to man within the near future. This chapter is called "Sex Selection in the Future: The Test-Tube Generation" and, among other things, will reveal how men may one day father offspring *without* women—offspring who will be identical to themselves in every detail!

The final chapter of this book—"Male and Female: Will There Still Be a Difference?"—looks at recent experiments in which the sex of animals has been changed *after* conc   s chapter also considers the possibility tha   l learn to mimic, through "genetic enginee   mber of interesting creatures that are able t   neir sexes at will—turning into females when   overabundance of males, and vice versa.

T   ver, takes us away from our immediate pr   ch is to try to force Mother Nature to be a li   equitable in her distribution of boys and   our own baby doctor may already have told you, Mother Nature *does* produce very nearly an equal number of boys and girls (the actual ratio in this country is something like 105 boys for every 100 girls), but while this equality exists in society as a whole *it does not prevail within family units*. The fact that the four Jones boys balance the four Smith girls may content Mother Nature, but it doesn't do much to cheer up the Joneses or the Smiths.

A Case History:
"A Boy at Last!"

Bill Martin put the telephone down and, in the words of his wife June, "bellowed out something that was halfway between an Indian war whoop and Tarzan's ape call."

Whatever it was, the Pennsylvania housewife remembers that it "brought little girls—including me—running from every corner of the house. And since there are five of us, that was a sight to behold: Becky, the youngest, tugging at Bill's leg, asking if it was time to play baseball again; Lana looking puzzled; and the two oldest, Molly and Lee, jumping up and down, screaming at him to tell us what the doctor had said. As for me, I was just standing there, six months pregnant, with a silly grin on my face. And then Bill, beaming like a lighthouse, said, 'It looks like we're going to have another man in the family,' and the girls just jumped all over

*him. From the top of the dogpile, Becky said something
like, 'Is Uncle Harry going to come stay with us again?'
That broke us all up, and one of the older girls, Molly, I
think, said, 'No, but Brother Billy is on his way.' "*

In order to understand just how the Martins knew
Brother Billy was on the way and, more important, how
they had planned for him (even before he was conceived), let's go back to the beginning.

"When we first married," writes June, a trim straw-
berry blonde of thirty-two, "we wanted to have our first
child right away. Bill was, and still is, a real sports
enthusiast, and, though he said time and again that he
would be happy with a healthy child of either sex, I
knew deep down that he had his heart set on a boy. And
at that point I was partial to little boys myself—maybe
because I grew up with three sisters and no brothers.
Right away we started trying to settle on names for the
baby we were planning. And the truth about how we
both felt came out when we realized that three fourths
of the names we came up with were for boys. Well, it
turned out Molly was our firstborn, and we didn't feel
even a twinge of disappointment. We were so happy to
have a healthy child of our own, we couldn't think about
anything else. It wasn't quite the same when Lee came
along next and we still didn't have a little boy.

"But then a couple years after that, Bill started talking
about completing the set, as he put it, with a boy. This
time we didn't even consider girls' names. It was going
to be William, Jr., and no mistake. I kept hinting to my

obstetrician how much Bill had his heart set on a boy, hoping, I guess, that he would give me some encouragement. Instead, he would only say that it is the man who determines the sex of the baby and that there was a 50–50 chance that we'd get what we wanted. Well, in a way, that made it a lot worse, because when Lana arrived several months later, Bill felt he had only himself to blame. Before that we had both thought it was the woman who determines the sex. And crazy as it seems to women, men seem to feel they're somehow lacking if they can't produce male offspring.

"After Lana, Bill was really depressed, though he was careful never to show it in front of the girls. And of course I was gloomy, too, mainly because it seemed like we had used up all our chances; we just didn't feel we could afford another child. It wasn't until nearly four years later—when Bill's business was finally operating solidly in the black—that we decided to have another try at it. By this time, of course, the relatives, the neighbors, everybody but the doctor, was offering us advice on how to go about having a boy. It was really incredible. One woman, who had just given birth to a boy, told me that her secret, passed along from her mother and so on, was alcohol. 'Get drunk as a loon the night you try, and you can't miss,' she said. Funny as that one was, it seemed a little more likely to work than the advice of one of my uncles, who told Bill to wear his boots to bed—and meant it!

"As for the doctors, they were no help at all. I pleaded

with my obstetrician to help us, but he said there was absolutely nothing he could do. 'You're a member of the 50–50 Club just like all the rest of us,' he said. I'll never forget that because it made me so mad. I told him the club was cheating me and I wanted out. He just shrugged his shoulders, and told me I'd better not have another child if I couldn't accept the chance—50 percent, he kept saying—that it would be a girl. Well, I finally told Bill I could take it if he could take it, and he said he could if I could. And we were both a little ridiculous for a few weeks—frantically trying to convince ourselves that a fourth girl wouldn't send us screaming to the hills. Hope springs eternal, as they say, and we decided to try one more time.

"As for the results, you guessed it. Nine months later we were the parents of a fourth little girl—Rebecca. I'll never forget Bill when he came into my room after delivery. There were tears in his eyes, but they weren't from joy.

"The next few months, I think, were the roughest we went through. Both Bill and I were more irritable around the children than ever before. Things weren't running too smoothly between the two of us, either. We just sort of stopped communicating. I began to feel a little sorry for myself. I even began to imagine that if it were the woman who determines the sex of the child I might not have been able to hold on to Bill. Sometimes it was all I could do to keep from reminding Bill that it was his fault, not mine, that we had four little girls

*in the family. And that would have been the worst thing
I could possibly have done—because Bill was only too
aware of that.*

"When I look back now I'm absolutely appalled at the
amount of anguish that can result from something like
the sex of one's children. At one point I was almost
fearing for our marriage—and I guess Bill was, too. Anyway, it was Bill, not me, who finally put a stop to all the
nonsense. One night after I'd been particularly hard
with one of the girls for some little thing, he said he'd
been acting like a fool and now he had me acting like
one, too. That broke the ice, and we vowed right there to
be happy with the four healthy children we had. From
then on things improved no end. The girls, of course,
turned into real little tomboys with Bill's encouragement, but most of them go through that stage anyway.

"We didn't even think about having another child
until four years later when one of Bill's sisters—a nurse in
New York City—sent us an article about a doctor who
had recently discovered a means of choosing sex. His
technique sounded so simple we couldn't believe it. Yet
this doctor reported success in more than 80 percent of
his cases, and some of them sounded just like ours. We
were so excited we called Bill's sister right away. One
thing in particular bothered us. The doctor had found
that most men whose offspring are all of one sex have
just had bad luck; with the proper conditions they
could produce children of the other sex, too. But the

article pointed out that a few men have the ability to produce only one sex.

"What if Bill was one of those few? The only way to find out, according to the article, was to have Bill's sperm examined under a special microscope. One thing led to another, and before I knew it Bill was back from New York with the good news. If we followed his directions—which involved a precoital douche and a timing procedure—the doctor said he thought we would have a good chance of conceiving a boy. He made no guarantees, but it was plain to us that we had finally broken out of the 50–50 Club. 'From here on out,' Bill said, 'we're 80 percenters.'

"I went off birth-control pills right away and, following directions, found myself pregnant six months later. By this time Molly was twelve and Lee ten, and they understood enough to share in the excitement with us. As I grew larger with each passing week, so did the suspense. When I was five months pregnant, Bill's sister suggested that I take advantage of a test that can determine the sex of the baby before it is born. When I found out how simple the test was, I agreed. We had to wait almost four weeks for the results, and those weeks seemed more like years. We waited and waited for that telephone call, wondering if it would prove us correct in thinking we were finally going to have a baby boy. The call that came through did just that."

Which brings us back to Bill's "ape call." At this writing, Bill, Jr. is a healthy three-month-old, and the

Martins now consider their family complete. June is almost as happy as Bill, so happy in fact that she has already forgiven the neighbor lady who, confident that the Martins were in for another girl, showered them with pink baby clothes the minute she heard June was pregnant again.

part I

HOW TO SELECT THE SEX OF YOUR CHILDREN *NOW*

1

Man Versus Mother Nature:
Early Attempts at Sex Selection

For centuries, man, determined to choose the sex of
his offspring, has indulged in a formidable number of
schemes and rituals—some imbued with the odor of
hobgoblin and humbug, others coated with the faint
patina of (crude) science. Although it has been the men,
ever eager to "prove" their virility and perpetuate their
names by begetting male children, who have been the
originators of most of these schemes, it has been the
women who have generally had to be the guinea pigs.
Consider, for example, the ordeal of some mothers in
the Middle Ages: if they wanted to please their husbands
and produce boys, they were advised by local "wise men"
to drink a gamey concoction of wine and lion's blood
mixed by an alchemist in the proper proportions. Then,
while an abbot prayed, they were directed to copulate

under a full moon. When the child turned out to be a girl in spite of these heroics, the wise men were usually ready with an explanation; perhaps a tiny cloud had suddenly obscured the masculinizing glow of the moon just at the moment of truth. In any event, despite countless failures, women faithfully went on guzzling lion's blood, and abbots fervently kept on praying. It is estimated that more than five hundred such "formulas" have been devised and recorded.

Many of our misconceptions about sex selection through the centuries can be attributed to the fact that the human body was off limits to anatomists for hundreds of years. Many of the animals that these investigators studied in place of man had two uteruses, so naturally, they assumed that man did, too. Thus it didn't seem farfetched at all when Parmenides of Elea, a Greek philosopher of the fifth century B.C., announced to the world that males develop in the right chamber and females in the left. This theory soon insinuated its way into the marital bed; wives were obliged to lie on their left side if a girl was desired and on their right in the more likely event that a boy was in demand. It was believed that this would cause the husband's semen to flow toward the appropriate uterine chamber.

Things became more complicated when Anaxagoras of the same era hypothesized that it was the testicles of the male that determined sex. The products of the right testicle produced boys while those of the left resulted in girls, according to this theory. (Note that in all of these theories, it is the *right* side—whether it be the right ovary, the right testicle, the right side of the body, or even the right side of the bed—that results in male offspring. Since right-handedness has always been associated with strength and justice, while left-handedness has traditionally been maligned as weak and evil, it doesn't take much imagination to understand the rationale behind these theories, all of which were concocted by men.)

Some of those who subscribed to both of these right-left theories found themselves in some rather strange positions. Some insisted that in order to beget male offspring *both* partners had to lie on their right sides during intercourse, so that right testicle and right uterus or ovary would be perfectly aligned. A variation on this theme was the idea that a man's testicles are of different sizes, and that the larger one produces the boys. Provided the husband could figure out which was the larger, he would then take care to lie on that side. One school of sex selection at that time made life considerably harder—this time for the men—by insisting that in addition to proper positioning, the right testicle should be firmly tied with a string, if a boy was wanted. It was Hippocrates, the Father of Medicine himself, who originated this knotty formula for male offspring.

Democritus and Aristotle, more than 2,000 years ago, had their own school of sex selection. According to their theories, women as well as men produce semen. If the female semen dominates, they said, the offspring will be female; if the male fluid prevails then a boy will result.

Democritus, who was a little more democratic in his outlook than some of his peers, said that while the dominant semen decided sex, a child's other characteristics were a "mosaic" formed through the intermingling of the male and female semen. A male child, he said, even though it inherited its genitals from its father, might still inherit its hands or face from its mother. In a crude way, this theory foreshadowed the modern chromosomal theory of development.

Aristotle, for his part, believed that semen dominance was a direct correlate of "vigor." The partner who is the more vigorous, particularly during the sex act, he said, determines the sex of the child. And he added that vigor was very often determined by the weather, some conditions favoring the wife and some the husband. He wrote that "more males are born if copulation takes place when a north wind than when a south wind blows, for the south wind is moister. Shepherds say that it makes a difference not only if copulation takes place during a north or a south wind, but even if the animals while copulating look toward the south or the north. So small a thing will sometimes turn the scale." One can only conclude that life was not easy for the ancients, who not only had to throw themselves right and left but north and south, too.

Later, the theory of "encasement" was popular. This quaint doctrine maintained that encased within the male and female sex glands are perfectly formed individuals of microscopic size. In turn, each of these "homonuclei," as they were called, was said to contain even smaller homonuclei, and so on in an unending series representing unending generations to come. When a homonucleus became large enough, it was supposedly extruded into the womb where, though already perfectly formed, it grew to a size sufficient to maintain life in the outside world. Various formulas for the selection of sex grew up around this theory, based on complicated notions about the ways in which the homonuclei are arranged one within another.

In more recent times, pseudoscientific theories have evolved, few enjoying more vogue than that of E. Rumley Dawson, a fellow of the Royal Society of Medicine, who before World War I popularized the notion that women—and women alone—are responsible for the sex of children. If the egg comes from the right ovary, he maintained, then the child will be a boy; if it comes from the left, it will be a girl. Dr. Dawson wrote countless articles and a book, *The Causation of Sex in Man*, in support of his theory, which, he said, could be used to select sex. According to his findings, the ovaries ovulate alternately, one this month and the other the next month. So, after the birth of the first child, he argued, it would be a simple matter to keep track of the cycles and to time intercourse accordingly. Hence, there was talk among women of "little-boy months" and "little-girl months." Apart from the fact that it has been proved that the male determines sex, Dr. Dawson erred, as well, in his contention that the ovaries always alternate in ovulation.

So far, most of the theories mentioned have a patina of science about them. Others rely on superstition and blind faith. Some reincarnation cults maintain that we simply alternate sexes in our various existences here on earth. If one is male this time around, he will be female next time—unless his soul is really set on one sex or the other; even then, according to these cults, individual choice will be denied if there is a shortage of one sex or the other.

Everywhere, it seems, boys are the preferred sex. Among the Ossets of the Central Caucasus, mothers-to-be spent their pregnancies in their home villages, separated from their husbands. If they gave birth to girls, they left the babies behind and returned to their men empty-handed, and nothing was said. But, if they produced sons they returned with their babies and heaps of gifts for the "successful" husbands. Similarly effective means of "selecting" sex have been used by a great many peoples including, at various times, the Eskimos and the Maori of New Zealand. During the early days of the British occupation, the Radshucmors of India killed nearly 10,000 newborn girls every year.

Less drastic measures were used by the young brides of the Pelew Islands, who dressed in male clothing before intercourse, believing that this would bring them male offspring. In Sweden brides-to-be slept with small boys on the eve of their weddings, again in order to ensure the birth of boys. In the Spessart Mountains of Germany, some husbands desiring male offspring still take an ax to bed with them and, during intercourse, chant to their wives, "Ruck, ruck, roy, you shall have a boy!" If they already have enough boys, the husbands will dispense with the ax and chant instead: "Ruck, ruck, rade, you shall have a maid!"

In parts of Austria, some peasants believe that a year with a good nut harvest will also yield an abundance of boys. To help things along, midwives frequently bury the afterbirth under a nut tree—thus supposedly making sure that the next child will be a boy. In parts of Czechoslovakia, the bride lets a small boy step on her hands, while in southern Yugoslavia the couple takes a boy to bed with them on their wedding night, again in the effort to beget a son.

In many of the Slavic countries, Hungary, and Bavaria, the wife is directed to pinch her husband's right testicle during intercourse. In the Italian province of Madena, the husband bites his wife's right ear. And in the backwoods of Pennsylvania, some men still hang their pants on the right side of the bed if they want a boy, on the left side if they want a girl.

Other folk theories maintain that boys will be conceived in the full of the moon, that the sex of the child will usually be that of the older parent, that the tides of the ocean determine sex, and that sweet foods will result in girls, while bitter or sour foods will produce boys. Some still believe that sex determination is a battle fought well into pregnancy, with male factors warring against female factors. In order to intervene in the "warfare" and tip the balance in favor of the desired sex, the expectant mother is advised to resort to a regimen of dietary "artillery," according to one folk theory. The most common prescription here calls for endless cakes and candies if one is hoping for female offspring and for "lots of good red meat" if one wants sons. It might be argued that this is at least an improvement over lion's blood.

2

Science to the Rescue:
The Saga of X and Y

Man's battle against Mother Nature has not been an easy one. Nor was it very successful until man began to turn his attention away from external forces (north winds, full moons, tides, and nut trees) and began focusing, instead, on *internal* factors within his own body. True enough, the ancient Greeks and a few others had come up with theories based on biological considerations, but these were predicated more on guesswork, prejudice, and wishful thinking than on scientific observation.

Man began to make real strides forward in his attempts at sex selection in 1827 when Karl von Baer identified the mammalian ovum or egg that is produced each month by the female ovary. Working with dogs, this pioneering biologist traced the development of the tiny embryos in the wombs of his laboratory animals back to the moment of conception. In the course of this, he dis-

covered that before the embryo—the combination of
sperm and egg—attaches itself to the lining of the uterus
it passes through one of the two Fallopian tubes that
open into the uterus. He was not certain that the embryo
had not simply been ejaculated into the female by her
mate during intercourse until he examined one of the
ovaries at the end of the Fallopian tube and discovered a
bulging follicle on its surface. Opening this, he discovered
a tiny yellowish speck, which under the microscope
turned out to be identical in appearance to the "ovules"
he had previously observed in the Fallopian tubes.

It wasn't until several years later—1841—that the
anatomist Rudolf von Kolliker conclusively established
that sperm originated within the tissue of the male
testes. This discovery was quickly followed by observation, in animal studies, of the actual penetration of the
egg cell by the much tinier sperm cell. The real nature
of fertilization in these studies, however, didn't become
apparent until the 1870's, when a series of researchers
concluded that the sperm and the egg combined in such
a way that each contributed about equally to the resulting embryo. In 1883, Pierre van Beneden, another European scientist, showed that this was precisely the case,
when he discovered that the central portion, or nucleus,
of both egg and sperm contain only half the number of
chromosomes that are present in the nuclei of all our
body cells.

Chromosomes are the microscopic, rodlike structures
that contain the even tinier genes, which determine the

color of our eyes, our facial features, the color of our skin, and all our other bodily characteristics. Every individual is made up of body cells and sex cells. The sex cells are the sperms or the eggs (ova). All the other cells—those that make up bone, skin, flesh, and so on—are called body cells. In man, each body cell contains forty-six of these rodlike chromosomes. Van Beneden's important discovery tells us that half of those chromosomes come from our mothers and half from our fathers, when their sex cells combine.

This discovery, however, still did not tell us just how Nature determines sex. We didn't know, for example, whether it was one of the mother's chromosomes or one of the father's chromosomes or a combination of the two that determined sex. The first suggestion that there might be *two types of sperm*—one carrying a female-producing chromosome and the other a male-producing chromosome—came in 1890. Microscopic studies of eggs indicated that the pairs of chromosomes within their nuclei were all perfectly matched. But similar studies showed that the sperm possessed *one* imperfectly matched pair.

One of the chromosomes in this odd pair was smaller than the other. Researchers quickly seized on this discrepancy as a possible explanation of the sex-determining mechanism. An American, C. E. McClung, in 1902, was the first to suggest that this seemingly mismatched pair constituted the sex chromosomes. It soon became fashionable to refer to the smaller of the two as the Y chromosome and to the larger as the X chromosome.

When the sperm cells underwent maturation and divided in half, it was hypothesized that the Y went into one of the newly formed sperm cells and the X into the other.

It should be understood that all of this work was with animal cells which, apart from the fact that they were readily available with no taboos attached, are also larger than human cells and therefore easier to study. Nonetheless, the principles these researchers developed were entirely sound and turned out to be as applicable to man as to animals. It was a study of the lowly mealwor first demonstrated that *the smaller Y chromoson duces males.* This came to light in 1905 when Dr. Stevens observed that half of the mature mealw sperm cells contain ten large chromosomes, while th other half contain nine large chromosomes and one small one (the Y chromosome). The ova all contain ten large chromosomes. Ova fertilized by sperms containing the Y chromosome all developed into males, while those fertilized by sperms containing the X chromosome yielded females without exception.

Momentous as this confirmation of McClung's theory was, decades passed before it became clear that the sex of humans is similarly determined. Human chromosomes are so small that it was not until 1956 that their number was firmly established at forty-six for each body cell and twenty-three for each sex cell. Indeed, no one had ever actually seen a human egg cell undergoing fertilization by a sperm cell until the latter part of the 1940's and the early 1950's, when Dr. John Rock of Harvard and Dr.

Landrum B. Shettles of Columbia University watched the miracle of conception on the stages of their microscopes. And although they could see the sperm penetrating the egg, they could not, in these living specimens, visualize the chromosomes themselves. They knew, however, from studies with stained and fixed specimens, that the X and Y chromosomes were there and that they determine sex. We shall see in the next chapter that Dr. Shettles has since discovered a means of visually identifying the X-carrying and the Y-carrying sperm cells in living specimens.

Let us pull together all the information science had gathered about human fertilization and sex determination by 1960 and put it to use in describing the conception of a baby. Will it be a boy or a girl? Follow along and we'll see:

First, the prelude to our drama, the preparation of the sperms and the eggs. At birth, a baby girl's ovaries contain more than half a million egg cells. That, of course, is far more than she will ever need. In fact, not more than 500 of these will mature during her lifetime to be released—one each month—from her ovaries. Why there are so many remains one of the mysteries of medical science.

Generally, though not always, the process of ovulation or egg production alternates between left and right ovary on a monthly cycle. Usually a week to twelve days after a woman's menstrual period, a tiny follicle (which simply means "little bag" in Latin) erupts from the surface of the ovary. This watery blister bursts open—sometimes causing the woman to feel a sharp twinge of pain—and the egg that it contains tumbles out and into the clutches of the lacy fimbriae or "fingers" of the Fallopian tube. These fingerlike structures draw the egg, which is no bigger than the point of a pin, into the tube. At this point the egg, the nucleus of which resembles in color and shape the yolk of a chicken's egg, is encased in a gelatinous mass of 4,000 to 5,000 "nurse" cells, which nourish and protect it during its first vulnerable hours outside the ovary.

As the egg bounces gently down the four-inch Fallopian tube, propelled by hairlike "cilia" that wave like tall grass in a soft breeze, the nurse cells gradually slough off and are dissolved by enzymes. At this point the placid egg is ready to meet her mate, the sperm cell, which is anything but placid.

While the egg is more than $\frac{1}{250}$ of an inch in diameter, the main body of the sperm is a mere $\frac{1}{8000}$ of an inch across, and its volume is only $\frac{1}{50,000}$ that of the egg. It has been estimated that all of the sperms necessary to produce the next generation in the United States could be contained in the space of a pin head, while the eggs necessary for the same job would fill a pint jar. During intercourse, the male, on the average, ejaculates 400 million sperm cells into the vagina. Why does the male produce and release so many of these microscopic creatures? Here we do know the answer—or at least part of it. It is because the vaginal environment is so hostile to the sperm cells, which are the smallest cells in the body. They die off by the millions shortly after they are released, slaughtered by the acid that abounds in the vagina.

Sperm cells resemble tadpoles with their rounded heads and long tails, which they use for propulsion, speeding (and considering their size, that's an accurate description) through the vaginal and cervical secretions at $\frac{1}{10}$ of an inch per minute. Taking their size into account, again, the 7-inch journey through the birth canal and womb to the waiting egg is equivalent to a 500-mile upstream swim for a salmon! Yet they often make this hazardous journey in under an hour, more than earning their title as "the most powerful and rapid living creatures on earth."

Only the fittest survive to pass through the cervix into the womb. Here they find a more hospitable environment, more alkaline than acidic. Still, many die along the way; others smash into the back of the womb or go up the wrong Fallopian tube. Many of those that go up the right one will miss the egg anyway, if only by a millionth of an inch. The idea that the egg exerts some magical power of attraction was disproved under Dr. Shettles' microscope. Those that hit the egg—and there are thousands of them that make it—do so blindly. Soon, though, the egg looks rather like a pincushion, except that in this case the "pins" beat their tails furiously, trying to drill into the egg. This is a sight never to be forgotten, one that Dr. Shettles calls the "dance of love" (see Figure 1).

Under the microscope one can see the sperms making heroic efforts to gain admittance to the egg's inner sanctum, which houses the nucleus and the chromosomes. Many are able to break through the egg's outer core, *but only one penetrates the interior,* tail and all, there to merge with the egg's nucleus and create a new human being. As soon as one sperm penetrates the nucleus, all others find the way to the heart of the egg blocked. Some unexplained mechanism within the egg apparently releases a chemical that renders the innermost portions of the egg absolutely impregnable once it has been fertilized by a single sperm. The egg's unsuccessful "suitors" wear themselves out "pounding at the door" and finally die of exhaustion.

As you will recall, the sperm carries twenty-three chromosomes and so does the egg. Twenty-two of these (in each) match up as pairs that determine all the bodily characteristics of the new individual—except for sex. The two remaining chromosomes decide the subject's sex. The female *always* contributes an X chromosome. If the sperm that penetrates the ovum also carries an X chromosome, the resulting individual will be XX, otherwise known as a girl. But if the sperm carries the Y chromosome, the baby will be XY which, to the geneticist, spells b-o-y.

And that's how Mother Nature does it.

3

Breakthrough:
Now You Can Choose

The name Landrum B. Shettles has already been mentioned several times in the course of this book, but in this chapter we share in his discovery, a discovery that promises to let you choose the sex of your next child. First, a further word of introduction: Dr. Shettles, M.D., Ph.D., D.Sc., is a member of the faculty of Columbia University's famed College of Physicians and Surgeons and of the staff of Columbia-Presbyterian Medical Center in New York City. He is a fellow of the American College of Obstetricians and Gynecologists and an internationally published expert on the physiology of human reproduction.

Those who have followed the career of Dr. Shettles will not be surprised to find him once again "tampering with Nature," as the fainthearted would have it. In the 1950's he stunned much of the world by repeatedly achieving test-tube conception: the fertilization of human ova by human sperm cells *outside the womb*. He grew one of his "test-tube babies" for six days, the point at which it would normally attach itself to the lining of the uterus. Segments of the religious press screamed "Monster!" and the Pope himself took the occasion of Dr. Shettles' attendance at the International Fertility Conference in Italy in 1954 to condemn those who "take the Lord's work" into their own hands. (No such objections have been raised about his current work in sex selection.)

Dr. Shettles felt that the work he was doing in the 1950's was both necessary and important, and so he continued with his research, thus contributing substantially to the study of human embryology. Thanks to the photographic record he made of his work, students for the first time were able to study *directly* the development of man from the moment of conception onward. Today, Dr. Shettles' photographs, or micrographs, as they are known—many of them considered classics— appear in his biological atlas, *Ovum Humanum*, in more than fifty textbooks on embryology, biology, and genetics and, in greatly enlarged form, in the American Museum of Natural History in New York, in the Museum of Science in Boston, and in the Academy of Sciences in Moscow.

Looking back on the furor that his work unleashed in the last decade, Dr. Shettles, now sixty, is particularly fond of recalling the "nice little old ladies" who would inquire indignantly about the origin of the human eggs he used in his experiments.

"Most of them I just poached," he would say. As for his scruples about growing a test-tube baby into a mature adult: "I have none," he says, smiling; "There's nothing I'd like better than to grow a beautiful lab assistant."

Dr. Shettles, M.D., Ph.D., egg poacher, "monster," sits in his cluttered office on the sixteenth floor of the Columbia-Presbyterian Medical Center in upper Manhattan and scuffs his feet back and forth with characteristic restlessness. He is recalling the night in the early 1960's when he made the discovery that may help millions select the sex of their offspring.

"Medical science had known for some time," he says, "that it is the male that determines the sex of the offspring. The man who leaves his wife because she brings him nothing but girls or nothing but boys is only kidding himself. If the man's fertilizing sperm carries an X chromosome, the child will be a girl; if it carries a Y it will be a boy."

The trouble is, he adds, doctors have always been unable to tell the difference between "male" sperm and "female" sperm. About all that was known was that the Y chromosome is smaller than the X. Dr. Shettles had long felt that this difference should be reflected in the overall size of the sperm heads. With ordinary microscopy, however, killed and permanently fixed sperm specimens failed to reveal the presence of two distinct sperm populations.

"Then one night," Dr. Shettles continues, "I decided to examine some *living* sperm cells under a phase-contrast microscope." The relatively new technique of phase-contrast microscopy throws eerie halos of light around dark objects, revealing details that ordinary microscopes miss. The living sperm cells on the stage of the microscope flashed through the field of vision like luminescent eels from the darkest depths of the ocean (see Figure 2). Dr. Shettles put them into slow motion by introducing a little carbon-dioxide gas into the specimen. The results were almost as electrifying as the "charged" sperm cells themselves: *almost immediately Dr. Shettles noticed that the sperms came in two distinct sizes and shapes.*

"I was so excited," he recalls, "that I ran upstairs and grabbed the first lab technician I could find. I had to show somebody what I'd found."

Now, after examining more than 500 sperm specimens in the same way and with the same results, he is convinced that the two sizes correspond to the two sexes: small, roundheaded sperms carry the male-producing Y chromosomes, and the larger, oval-shaped type carry the female-producing X chromosomes (see Figure 3). He noticed that in most cases the round sperms far outnumbered the oval-shaped sperms, a state of affairs that is compatible with the fact that 110 to 170 boys are conceived for every 90 to 100 girls, and that for every 100 female births there are about 105 male births. In

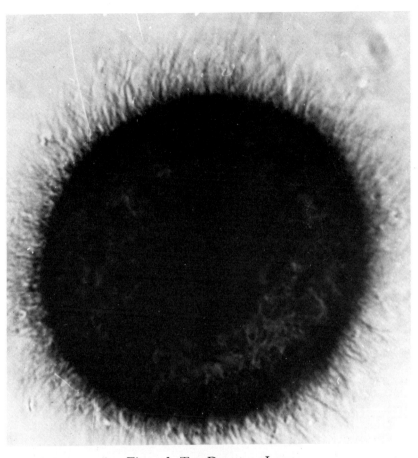

Figure 1: THE DANCE OF LOVE
Thousands of sperm, looking like pins in a pincushion, fight for admission
to the egg's inner sanctum. Only one will make it.

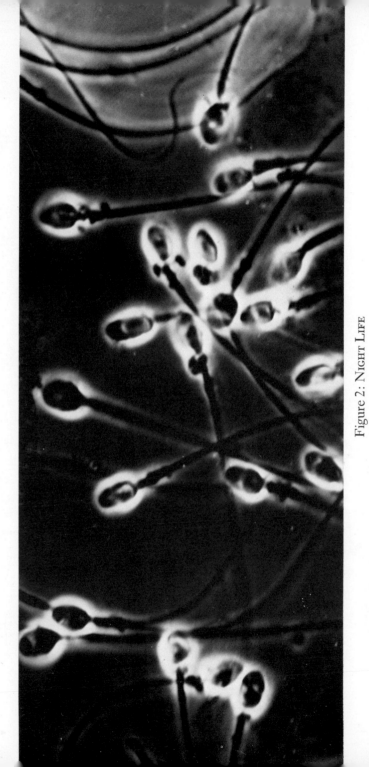

Figure 2: NIGHT LIFE

Under the phase-contrast microscope, sperm cells are shrouded with surreal halos of light.

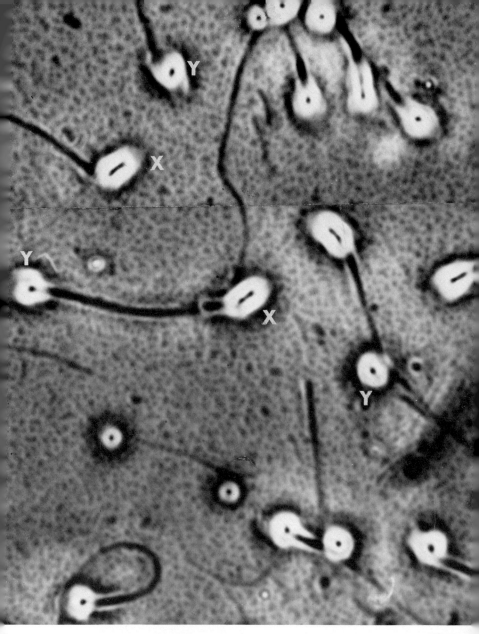

Figure 3: BOY OR GIRL?
X marks the female, Y the male.

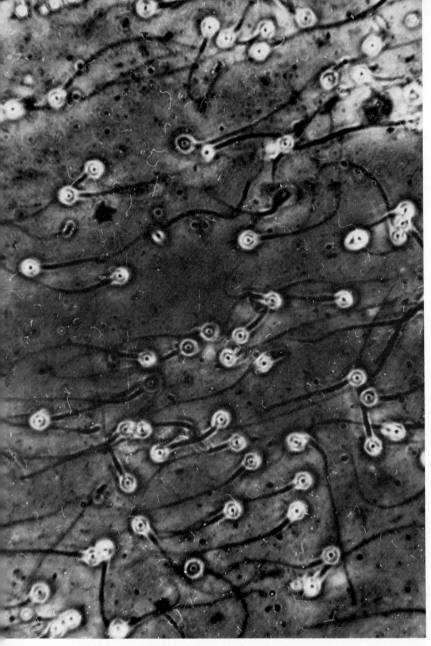

Figure 4: AND NOT A GIRL IN SIGHT
The donor of this sperm sample, populated by nothing but Y's, comes from a family that for 256 years has produced almost nothing but boys. Such cases are extremely rare.

terms of longevity, resistance to disease and stress, adaptability to environment, and so on, it has long been conceded, at least by scientists, that the male is the weaker of the two sexes. The male may have more muscular strength than the female but he lacks her staying power. This fact now appears to be borne out even at the most elemental level; the male-producing sperms begin with a substantial head start in terms of numbers (perhaps a 2 to 1 margin, because of an extra cell division), but end up only slightly ahead of the female-producing sperms.

With this much to go on, Dr. Shettles began checking the family histories of the men whose sperm he had examined. He failed to find anyone who produced only the oval-shaped female sperms, but he did encounter some specimens which contained almost nothing but the roundheaded variety. In each of the latter cases his physiological sleuthing revealed a man who had produced nothing but male offspring. In cases in which the long-headed sperms prevailed, he generally found fathers surrounded by little girls (and wives who wanted boys). Dr. Shettles stressed here, however, the rarity of cases in which the husband produces only sperm that is predominantly of one type. And even in cases in which a man may produce considerably more sperm of one type than the other *he can very often still produce offspring of both sexes,* provided he follows certain procedures, which we will discuss later in this chapter. (Just why, in these rare cases, some men "favor" one type of sperm over the other is still not understood, though genetic factors seem to play an important role The point to remember is that a strong predisposing factor, genetic or otherwise, to produce one sex or the other is absent in most males, and even where present, it can often be overcome. Individuals who have repeatedly fathered children of the same sex are more often the victims of bad luck than of genetics.)

In his laboratory, Dr. Shettles fondly flicks through the pages of his scientific papers, pointing to pictures of his patients' sperm.

"What do you notice about this one?" he will ask, and you must acknowledge that it contains "nothing but roundheaded ones" (see Figure 4). And then he regales you with the genealogy of its donor, who comes from a family that for 256 years has produced almost nothing but male offspring, the "almost" being reserved for the two females that came along during those two and half centuries. Those two women, he points out, displayed marked hirsutism (body hair) and masculinity. Then, a crafty smile creasing his face, Dr. Shettles asks you to examine yet another micrograph. You remark that this one is populated with both types of sperm, in fairly equal numbers, at which the doctor admits that the specimen is his own and that he is the proud father of four girls and three boys.

After making his discovery, Dr. Shettles published his findings in the prestigious scientific journal *Nature* and suddenly found himself in a new controversy. Lord

Rothschild, a British physiologist, apparently suffering from the well-known "British First" syndrome (that is, British scientists desperately trying to beat their American counterparts to significant discoveries), went on television to characterize Dr. Shettles' findings as "a lot of tripe." Lord Rothschild attempted to support his evaluation with a curious list of objections, which, to some observers, seemed only to reveal Lord Rothschild's lack of expertise in dealing with phase-contrast microscopy. *The New York Times* subsequently published a full-scale rebuttal by Dr. Shettles in which it was reported that "twenty-five trained observers have confirmed the presence of two distinct types of sperm heads in the specimens under study at Columbia and that two specialists had independently repeated the experiments and had also confirmed them."

Typical of Lord Rothschild's objections to Dr. Shettles' presentation in *Nature* was one in which he said, "Dr. Shettles reproduces a photograph of what is alleged to be human sperm. This head is no less than thirty microns long, whereas the average human sperm head is five microns long."

In answer, Dr. Shettles said, "Lord Rothschild apparently was trying to make scientific measurements on the basis of the printed illustration in the magazine. Under those circumstances it is remarkable that he came as close to the real measurements as he did."

All of this is mentioned simply to indicate that not *everybody* has agreed with Dr. Shettles' findings. Nor does Dr. Shettles claim any scientific infallibility. But he does stand on his record, on the observations he has made in the laboratory and, most important, on his results to date. Moreover, as we proceed, we shall see that other researchers have provided some impressive corroboration of Dr. Shettles' work.

As soon as he had dealt with this British broadside, Dr. Shettles had only one thing in mind: to find some means of exploiting the new knowledge he had acquired to help parents choose the sex of their children. As he put it, he was tired of telling patients that they would just have to be content with what Nature decided to give them. But *how* to exploit this new knowledge? Well, since there definitely seemed to be a difference in the overall size of the two types of sperms, he reasoned, there must be other differences, as well. Perhaps one type was stronger than the other or faster—or both. Perhaps one type could survive longer in a certain environment than could the other. There were all sorts of intriguing possibilities that could lead to a means of selecting sex—simply by interfering, even slightly, with the environment in which the sperm seeks out the egg.

From the start it seemed fairly certain that the larger, female-producing sperms (now called gynosperms) must be more resistant than the other type. Otherwise, why should there be nearly twice as many of the smaller, boy-producing variety (known as androsperms) in the ejaculate of the average male? Why, in other words, was there this apparent extra division (and hence doubling) of the androsperms, if not to compensate for some inferiority in coping with the environment beyond the male reproductive tract? This "inferiority," as suggested earlier, is borne out all through life: there are far more stillbirths and miscarriages of male children than of female; more boys than girls die during infancy; women are more resistant than men to numerous diseases, have longer life spans, and so on. No wonder the androsperms require a substantial head start—even then the boys end up only slightly out in front of the girls, in terms of the number born each year.

What accounts for the greater slaughter of androsperms within the womb? To find out, Dr. Shettles began studying the environment that exists inside the vagina and uterus at about the time of conception. He took transparent capillary tubes and filled them with cervical and vaginal secretions. Then he turned millions of sperms loose at the opening of the tubes and watched their activity through his microscope.

"It was a little like watching the races at Belmont," he said, calling his capillary tubes "physiological racetracks."

When the secretions in the tubes were more acidic than alkaline, the gynosperms seemed to prevail. Their greater bulk seemed to protect them from the acid for much longer periods than their little brothers were able to survive. But when the tubes were filled with cervical mucus that had been removed from a woman very close to the time of ovulation, the smaller androsperms were clear-cut winners every time. Why? Because the ovulatory mucus is highly alkaline, an environment that favors the androsperms.

Now to clarify: acid inhibits both gynosperms *and* androsperms, but it harms the androsperms first and most, cutting them out of the herd and thus out of competition. Alkaline secretions are kind to both types of sperm and generally enhance the chances for fertilization. (That is why a woman's body chemistry becomes increasingly alkaline as the moment of ovulation approaches.) But in the absence of hostile acids the androsperms are able to use the *one* advantage they have over their sisters: the speed and agility that their small, compact heads and long tails give them.

Here Dr. Shettles had some very important information indeed. As a gynecologist he knew that the environment within the vagina is generally acidic, while the environment within the cervix and uterus is generally alkaline. And he knew that the closer a woman gets to ovulation the more alkaline her cervical secretions become. He knew, also, as a result of his "racing" experiments, that female-producing sperms are likely to outlast their male-producing counterparts in an acidic environment and, as a result of their strength and resistance (some would simply say their tough hides), manage to fight their way to the egg first. (He checked out this resistance theory in other ways; by heating the capillary tubes, for example, he was able to observe the greater staying power of the gynosperms. All of the sperm cells died from the heat eventually, but the androsperms died first.) In an alkaline environment he knew that the androsperms were clearly superior, able to use their agility to the fullest.

All of this told him that *timing of intercourse* is a critical factor in choosing the sex of children. His findings suggested that intercourse at or very close to the time of ovulation, when the secretions are most alkaline, would very likely result in male offspring. Intercourse two or three days before the time of ovulation, on the other hand, when an acid environment still prevails, would be likely to yield female offspring.

Already some readers, concerned about pinpointing the exact time of ovulation, may be wondering what might be the effects of frequent intercourse, starting about three days before the suspected time of ovulation. Could this "shotgun" approach to the timing problem be a means of begetting a boy, since intercourse would occur at least once at or near the time of ovulation? The answer is almost certainly negative, for this reason: gynosperms from the first intercourse in the series could, because of their superior staying power, still be lurking in the Fallopian tube three days after being deposited there, but it is very unlikely that there could still be any androsperms alive or in condition to fertilize the egg. Subsequent intercourse would probably be futile, since fertilization—by a girl-producing sperm—would already have taken place by the time male reinforcements arrived at the time of ovulation. The timing factor and the means of pinpointing ovulation are described in more detail later in this chapter and the following one.

Certain now that he was on the right track, Dr. Shettles began looking through scientific and historical literature to try to discover further confirmation of his findings. He found that Orthodox Jews produce significantly more male offspring than does the general population. To find out why this might be so, he began consulting rabbis and poring over the Talmud, a compilation of Jewish beliefs, laws, manners, and customs that was completed between the fourth and sixth centuries A.D. One of the passages he found was this: "The determination of sex takes place at the moment of cohabitation. When the woman emits her semen before the man [meaning when she experiences orgasm before her husband], the child will be a boy. Otherwise, it will be a girl." If a boy was desired, the Talmud directed the husband to "hold back" until his wife experienced orgasm. Before considering this further, let us go on to the second point that Dr. Shettles found in Orthodox Jewish law: that women must not engage in intercourse during their "unclean" period (menstruation) or for one week thereafter.

Both of these directives coincided very neatly with Dr. Shettles' findings, explaining why Orthodox Jews have more male offspring than the rest of the population. Orgasm is the less important of the two factors, but it can play a part in sex selection; female orgasm, Dr. Shettles has found, helps provide additional alkaline secretions. Of course, many women (perhaps 40 percent) never experience orgasm. These women should not be alarmed nor think that their chances to conceive boys are diminished. Female orgasm is probably desirable, but it is certainly optional, for there are other ways, as we shall see, of increasing the alkalinity that favors male off-spring. The other point—abstaining from intercourse until at least a week after the conclusion of menstruation—is more significant, for this puts coitus at a point very close to the time of ovulation in most women, the point at which the secretions are most alkaline. And so it is, Dr. Shettles concluded, that Orthodox Jews beget many male offspring.

Dr. Shettles also sifted through the data on artificial insemination (a technique that accounts for several thousand live births each year in this country). He knew that doctors specializing in artificial insemination try to pinpoint the time of ovulation in their patients so that fertilization can be achieved on the first try, if possible. This is simply more economical and less traumatizing for the patient. It occurred to Dr. Shettles that an un-intended side effect of this practice ought to be an abundance of male offspring. In a series of several thousand births achieved by artificial insemination, he found that the sex ratio was 160 boys for every 100 females. In another series, 76 percent were boys, and 24 percent were girls!

Elated that his hunch seemed to be correct, Dr.

Shettles began startling some of his patients by telling them that they no longer had to rely on the whims of Mother Nature—at least not entirely—when it came to the sex of their children. He also began working at about this time with Dr. Sophia Kleegman, a professor of gynecology at New York University's Medical School and director of its Infertility Clinic. Dr. Kleegman has long been a leader in the field of artificial insemination. She began sending samples of her donors' sperm to Dr. Shettles—for analysis under the phase-contrast microscope. Today both Dr. Shettles and Dr. Kleegman are enjoying a high rate of success in helping their patients choose the sex of their children. Both have attained records of 80 percent success, and Dr. Shettles believes that 90 or 95 percent is not out of the question.

Recently, Dr. Shettles summarized his findings to date for a scientific publication.* An excerpt of this summary, along with his two "recipes" for selecting sex, follow.

The difference in shape and size, as well as the correspondence of the overall ratio of sperm type with the conception rate by sex, suggest that other factors are operating, as well as pure numbers. Speed is one such factor and would seem to favor the smaller Y-bearing sperm. Since these are of less mass than the larger X-bearing sperm, they should be able to migrate through the reproductive secretions at the time of ovulation at a greater speed with the same amount of energy, thus making one of them more likely to effect fertilization. When tested in a capillary tube filled with

* *International Journal of Gynecology and Obstetrics*, Baltimore, Md.

ovulation cervical mucus over a distance of one foot, the small-headed sperm invariably wins the race.

Continence [meaning abstention from intercourse] or lack thereof is another factor which could favor one or the other type, depending on the circumstances. . . . Continence is associated with an increased frequency of roundheads [androsperm]. Oligospermia [low sperm count] is associated with female offspring. In men with sperm counts of 20 million cc and under [20 million sperms per cubic centimeter of fluid], the likelihood of female offspring varies inversely with the count. With a sperm count of a million or less, only female offspring resulted. . . . This is indicative of the X-chromosome-bearing sperm [female-producing] being the survival of the fittest.

A third factor is longevity, which seems to favor the X-bearing sperm. When the egg is ready for fertilization, this factor may be unimportant, but it is possible for fertilization to occur by a robust sperm which has survived over a period of days within the tube.

Interrelated with the above is differential environment within the cervix before and at time of ovulation. At the time of ovulation the cervical mucus is, among other things, most abundant, most alkaline, of lowest viscosity, and most conducive to sperm penetration and survival. In contrast, the more acid environment within the cervix until a day or so before ovulation is unfavorable to sperm. During this time only the more fit (female) sperm have a chance for survival. The potential to have male and female offspring obviously varies greatly among men. Utilization of each lot of reproductive talents, so to speak, is governed greatly by the timing of coitus in relation to ovulation.

The findings outlined above have enabled Dr. Shettles to formulate two procedures—one to be used if female offspring is desired, the other if a male is wanted. These procedures, he says, can be used in the home *without* prior semen analysis. The number of cases in which men are able to produce only one sex or, because their sperm counts are so low, are able to produce only females, is too insignificant to warrant the expense and inconvenience of such tests, which most doctors are not yet equipped to carry out yet, anyway.

The Procedure for Female Offspring

1. Intercourse should cease two to three days before ovulation.

2. Intercourse should be *preceded*, on each occasion, by an acid douche consisting of two tablespoons of *white* vinegar to a quart of water. The timing might be enough to ensure female offspring, but the douche—which is completely harmless—makes success all the more likely, since the acid environment immobilizes the androsperms.

3. If the wife normally has orgasm she should try to avoid it. Orgasm increases the flow of alkaline secretions, and these could neutralize or weaken the acid environment that enhances the chances of the gynosperms.

4. The face-to-face or "missionary" position should be assumed during intercourse. Dr. Shettles believes that this makes it less likely that sperms will be deposited

directly at the mouth of the cervix, where they might escape the acid environment of the vagina.

5. Shallow penetration by the male at the time of male orgasm is recommended. Again, this helps make certain that the sperm are exposed to the acid in the vagina and must swim through it to get to the cervix.

6. No abstinence from intercourse is necessary, until after the final intercourse two or three days before ovulation. We have seen that a low sperm count increases the possibility of female offspring, so frequent intercourse, prior to the final try two or three days before ovulation, cannot hurt and may actually help. This may be why Dr. Shettles says, "Having girls is more fun."

The Procedure for Male Offspring

1. Intercourse should be timed as close to the moment of ovulation as possible.

2. Intercourse should be *preceded,* on each occasion, by a baking-soda douche, consisting of two tablespoons of baking soda to a quart of water.

3. Female orgasm is not necessary but is desirable. If a woman normally experiences orgasm, her husband should time his to coincide with hers or let her experience orgasm first.

4. Vaginal penetration from the rear is the recommended position. This, Dr. Shettles says, helps ensure deposition of sperm at the entrance of the womb rather than in the two spaces adjacent to it, the cul-de-sac and

the posterior fornix. This is desirable because the secretions within the cervix and womb will be highly alkaline, more so even than the vagina, in spite of the alkaline douche, and an alkaline environment is most favorable to androsperms.

5. Deep penetration at the moment of male orgasm will help ensure deposition of sperm close to the cervix.

6. Prior abstinence is necessary; intercourse should be avoided completely from the beginning of the monthly cycle until the day of ovulation. This helps ensure maximum sperm count, a factor favoring androsperms.

"All of this means," Dr. Shettles observes, "that if the first intercourse of the month takes place right at ovulation time, when cervical fluid increases tenfold and is very alkaline, the male sperm will race through like a cab going through Broadway on a green light." If, however, intercourse takes place two or three days before ovulation, most of the male sperms will be incapacitated by the time the egg arrives.

"For the female sperm," Dr. Shettles continues, "it's like flying into LaGuardia on a foggy night. They have to hover around and wait for the signal. Then they zoom right in."

Dr. Shettles, again, does not *guarantee* that these procedures will be successful on *every* occasion. But, as he puts it, "the procedures are safe and simple. There's nothing distasteful about them, nothing any religious body has objected to. They can be carried out in the home and they are entirely harmless. Clinical results show at least 80 percent success. And I believe that if the couple is conscientious with the douche and the timing that they can achieve success 85 to 90 percent of the time."

4

Letters from Home:
Questions and Answers

Following the publication of a brief article on sex selection in *New York* Magazine, the gist of which was picked up by the wire services and disseminated around the world, hundreds of letters poured in, some addressed to the author, some to Dr. Shettles. The letters were from people in many different countries and from varied walks of life. Some were scribbled in pencil on brown paper, others had the imprint of the IBM electric; some were from doctors, lawyers, and professors, others were from shopkeepers, construction workers and, of course, mothers. A surprising number were from husbands. But varied as the sources were, the requests were almost always the same: "Help us get more information so that we can choose the sex of our next baby."

Many women wrote to recount the trials they had been through in trying to find a doctor willing to help them—

or even sympathize with them—in their efforts at sex selection.

One woman from Virginia wrote Dr. Shettles as follows: "I'm the mother of three boys, and I love them dearly, but at the same time my husband and I very much want a little girl. The enclosed article about your work has provided us with our first ray of hope. . . . However, the article was brief and, since we needed more information, I asked my gynecologist to help. I also went to a urologist to see if he could do the sperm analysis for my husband. He just laughed at me and said I was wasting my time. When I told him I thought he might be a little behind the times he called me a 'silly, immature girl' and said I should be happy with whatever Nature gives me in the way of children. I was so embarrassed I could have died. Now I'm more angry than embarrassed, since both of these doctors have children of both sexes. They have no idea about the deep hurt that can come from having children of the same sex over and over."

Perhaps the most predictable letter came from a young mother in Kansas City, Mo., who wrote: "Thank you for making me the winner of a battle that's been raging between my husband and myself for the last two years. We have three adorable daughters but have wanted a boy from the start. My husband has needled me ever since we got married about not being able to have a boy. His mother told him it was the woman who determines the sex of the baby. The two of them kept telling me this until I almost believed it myself, though I always thought the man must be at least halfway responsible. I could have cleared this up a long time ago, I guess, by asking my doctor, but I thought it would make me sound so dumb. Anyway, after I saw this article I showed it to my husband right away and told him that if he wants a son so bad he's going to have to have his sperm analyzed. And if he can't produce any Y's he's had it!"

Here is a case of poetic justice—or something approaching it. After centuries in which men cast off wives who couldn't produce male heirs, it looks as if the tables may have been turned.

What follows is a series of questions taken from similar letters, accompanied by answers based on Dr. Shettles' findings.

Q: "Since determining the time of ovulation is the most important aspect in trying to choose sex, could you help us get more information on this? My own periods are rather irregular; what can I do?"

A: There are a number of ways of determining the time of ovulation. Generally, women are told to keep a temperature chart. Your own doctor is familiar with this procedure and can instruct you in it. This procedure involves a special but inexpensive thermometer scored in tenths of a degree so that even tiny variations aren't missed. Temperature is taken orally each day before getting out of bed in the morning and then is recorded on the chart. This should commence at the beginning of menstruation and continue until the end of the monthly cycle. Typically, temperature will remain about even throughout menstruation and will probably rise or fall two or three tenths of a degree over the next several days. A sudden dip of perhaps two tenths of a degree—or more—in temperature over a period of a day usually indicates that ovulation is at hand, though no one is certain whether ovulation takes place at the bottom of the dip or as it begins to rise again. The temperature will rise sharply again, usually within a day, and remain high, indicating that ovulation has taken place. Women who rely on these charts should maintain records for two or, preferably, three or four months before using them for sex selection. If the woman is emotionally upset, ill, or if she smokes, eats, or moves about before taking her temperature each morning, the charts are not likely to be very accurate.

Because of the instability of the temperature approach, Dr. Shettles recommends a simpler, newer, and more accurate procedure. This involves the purchase of a fertility test kit (available at most drugstores for about $7) or, for less money, but equally good, a little roll of something called Tes-Tape, also available in most drugstores without prescription. Tes-Tape is simply a roll of special yellow paper that comes in a Scotch Tape-type dispenser; the tape turns varying shades of blue and green when exposed to glucose. Tes-Tape was designed to help diabetics test the amount of sugar that accumulates in their urine. That sugar is glucose. And in the

1950's Dr. Shettles and some of his co-workers discovered that glucose is also abundant in cervical mucus at the time of ovulation.

To use the Tes-Tape properly, Dr. Shettles suggests the following procedure: beginning at the end of menstruation, start off each day by tearing off a three-inch strip of tape. Bend the strip over the index finger (you'll have to sacrifice that fingernail temporarily) and secure it to the finger with a small rubber band. Now guide the finger into the vagina so that the tip of your finger and the tape make contact with the cervix. How do you know when you are touching the cervix? Dr. Shettles says that it feels something like the tip of your nose. Hold the finger gently up against the cervix for ten to fifteen seconds, then withdraw it. Note the color of the tape at the tip of your finger. Early in the cycle it probably won't change color at all. Or it might change to a light green. As you approach ovulation, each new tape will be darker and darker where it has made contact with the cervical mucus (which, you remember, becomes increasingly alkaline as ovulation approaches). To determine when ovulation is about to take place, consult the color chart on the Tes-Tape or fertility kit dispenser; when the color matches that of the darkest color on the scale (a deep, greenish blue) you will know that ovulation is at hand.

You will notice that the Tes-Tape chart is coded for the urine test, but it works for ovulation as well. Dr. Shettles recommends that you experiment with the procedure through three or four cycles before using it for the critical intercourse. In this way you can determine the day on which you normally ovulate and what color the tape is two or three days before it turns its darkest hue. This latter information will be important if you are trying for a girl. Keep careful records of the approximate color that turns up each day. Five different color bars are indicated on the Tes-Tape chart, so you may want to number these one through five, starting with yellow, and jot down the applicable number each day.

Some women prefer to use the Tes-Tape and the temperature technique; if you can get the two to coincide you can be that much more certain that you have pinned down your time of ovulation. If temperature is highly erratic, however, it is best to rely on the Tes-Tape. Also, it is wise to test the cervical mucus two or three times a day as it approaches its darkest hue, so that if a boy is wanted you can time coitus as closely as possible to ovulation. If you feel that you are using the Tes-Tape or fertility kit (which comes equipped with an applicator) incorrectly, consult your doctor.

Q: "My doctor tells me that I have *Mittelschmerz*. How reliable an indicator of ovulation is this?"

A: According to both Dr. Shettles and Dr. Kleegman, *Mittelschmerz* is the best indicator of all. For those not familiar with this harmless, and in our case helpful, ailment, it is a pain that is felt in the lower abdomen, often on the right side, at the time of ovulation. Some women feel a sharp twinge of pain at the precise moment that the egg bursts out of its follicle. Some experience a small amount of bleeding at the same time. If you have similar midcycle pains or bleeding, check with your doctor; it could be *Mittelschmerz*. About 15 percent of all women have these precise pains and thus are able to pinpoint ovulation almost to the exact second. In other women the pains are nonexistent or vague. Some women who have *Mittelschmerz* have been operated on for acute appendicitis—or what the doctor thought was acute appendicitis—only to go on experiencing the pains month after month. Dr. Kleegman always alerts her patients to these pains and, in fact, has taught 35 percent of her patients to bring the pain out by practicing what she calls the "bounce test." From the ninth day of the cycle, both morning and night, the woman is instructed to bounce on a hard surface, such as a wooden chair, by sitting down abruptly three or four times. If she feels the pain she should note the day and repeat the test during the next cycle to see if a pattern emerges.

Q: "What exactly is the 'stretch test' I read about?"

A: The cervical mucus is generally thick and rather milky in appearance. But it becomes increasingly thin and clear as ovulation approaches, until it reaches the consistency and transparency of raw egg white. At ovulation time it can be stretched easily, and this is where the "stretch test" comes from. This test, however, is usually administered only by doctors, though some women may notice the changing nature of their cervical mucus and use this to help determine the time of ovulation.

For the normal woman whose cycle runs anywhere from twenty-eight to thirty-five days, Dr. Shettles recommends using Tes-Tape or one of the fertility kits to determine time of ovulation. He recognizes, however, that temperature charting and observation of the color and consistency of the cervical mucus can be useful. Women with vague midcycle pains that continue over a number of days and never reach a definite peak, should also use one of the other methods (besides *Mittelschmerz*) for pinpointing ovulation. Even women with well-defined *Mittelschmerz* should try to confirm with one of the other tests.

Q: "Is it true that most women ovulate on the fourteenth day of the cycle?"

A: The fourteenth day is often cited as the most likely day because it falls in the middle of the twenty-eight-day cycle. This cycle, however, is an average; not every woman ovulates on the fourteenth day. Some studies show that the greatest number of women ovulate on day twelve, and that others ovulate on day thirteen, fourteen, or fifteen. A few women ovulate on day six, or even earlier. Most women ovulate between days eleven and fifteen, but each woman must determine for herself her ovulation time.

Q: "As a man, I must object to your statement that the male is solely responsible for the sex of the child. He contributes the male- and female-producing sperm, but isn't it also true that conditions within the woman can favor one or the other type of sperm?"

A: Looked at in this way, it is a fact that women share in the responsibility. The woman whose secretions tend to be highly acidic, for example, puts her husband's male-producing sperm at a real disadvantage and, in this sense, helps "select" females. Similarly, some women, using various bits of misinformation, may insist on a particular timing for coitus that consistently favors one sex or the other. One woman, for example, who has three girls and no boys, wrote that she had been told that when trying to conceive, she should engage in the first intercourse of the cycle exactly five days after menstruation. It is not possible to assess the day on which this woman ovulates on the basis of a single letter, but it does seem unlikely that it would be as early as day ten. It seems considerably more probable that she ovulates on day twelve—two days after intercourse. At that point only the more sturdy gynosperms, which produce females, would still be able to fertilize the egg.

In another case along these same lines, however, it was the man who appeared to be responsible for an abundance of girls. As a truck driver, he was home only every other week, a circumstance that for three years caused him to have intercourse with his wife during the earliest portion of his wife's fertile period. Last intercourse was never later than the end of the twelfth day. As it turned out, his wife ovulated on the fourteenth day and never before; hence three little girls.

Q: "Can the husband's or wife's age have anything to do with the sex of their children?"

A: The sperm count of some males declines with age and this, as we noted earlier, can result in more female offspring. Similarly as a woman ages, the cyclical nature of her body chemistry slowly breaks down, and the quantity and quality of her cervical secretions (which tend to be alkaline) diminish over the years. This deterioration tends to favor female offspring. And it is true that older couples do produce more female offspring than do younger people. One study showed that women of about fifteen, twenty, thirty, and forty years of age had offspring with sex ratios of 163, 120, 112, and 91 males, respectively, for every 100 females. The older woman, however (if she wants male offspring), can overcome this disadvantage by using the alkaline douche and timing procedures outlined in the previous chapter.

Q: "How soon before intercourse should the douche be taken?"

A: The douche should be used within a few minutes before intercourse. In the case of the baking-soda (or bicarbonate of soda) douche, the solution should be permitted to stand for fifteen minutes before use. This allows the soda to become completely dissolved. The vinegar—which should be the white variety—will mix with the water immediately and can be used at once.

Q: "Should the douche be applied with a syringe-type applicator?"

A: Dr. Shettles recommends the hot-water-bottle applicator. Let the fluid flow under the force of gravity alone.

Q: "We are a little confused about the timing. What happens if intercourse takes place a few hours *after* ovulation? Will a boy or a girl be the most likely result?"

A: According to Dr. Shettles' findings, a boy will be most likely during the six or seven hours immediately following ovulation, since the cervical secretions are still generally very abundant and highly alkaline during this period. Remember to test the cervical secretions—using the Tes-Tape or the fertility kit tape—just before intercourse (and always before douching) to see whether the secretions are still highly alkaline, provided you want a boy. If they are alkaline, it will not matter if ovulation has already taken place. When the tape is its darkest color your chances for a boy are the best.

Q: "How long do the sperm and egg live?"

A: Sperm cells have been known to survive for up to a week inside the womb. This, however, is extremely rare. Generally, the female-producing sperm will survive no more than two or three days. Male-producing sperm cells usually die within twenty-four hours. The egg itself often lives for only twelve hours, rarely more than twenty-four hours.

Q: "We are trying for a girl and don't want to take any unnecessary chances. We have decided to time intercourse for three days prior to ovulation, but our doctor tells us that this may keep us from getting pregnant at all. Is this true?"

A: Dr. Shettles notes that the further away from ovulation that one times intercourse, the more difficult it is to achieve pregnancy. But it is also true that when one does achieve pregnancy in these cases, the offspring is very likely to be a girl. Since the couple in question doesn't want to take "unnecessary chances," it is wise to time intercourse well ahead of ovulation. If, after three or four months, they have still not achieved pregnancy on this schedule, they should move to a two-and-a-half-day interval and then, if that also fails, to a two-day interval. At two days it is still far more likely that female offspring will result (provided the other procedures are also followed). But the couple wanting a girl has nothing to lose by starting out with the more cautious three-day interval. Pregnancy can and does occur in a significant number of cases under these circumstances.

It might be a good idea to reiterate here some of the clinical results of these timing procedures. "With exposure to pregnancy 2 to 24 hours before ovulation," Dr. Kleegman reports, "the babies were predominantly male (78 percent). With exposure to pregnancy 36 or more hours before ovulation, the babies were predominantly female." Dr. Kleegman also reports that women who were using the rhythm method of birth control but still became pregnant (from intercourse between days 4 and 7 of the cycle) gave birth to female babies 80 percent of the time. In another study, Dr. Shettles reported that one group of 22 couples who wanted female offspring took up to six months to conceive by consistently timing intercourse two to three days before ovulation. "Of 22 off-spring," he notes, "19 were girls. In a group of 26 women anxious to have boys, the first coitus occurred at the time of ovulation or within 12 hours thereafter. To these women, 23 boys were born."

Q: "We have given birth to three boys and no girls. My husband would like to have his sperm analyzed to see whether he is able to produce female sperm before we make another attempt. Can you tell us whether there is a center in our locality that can do this?"

A: There are only a few doctors in the United States equipped to carry out these analyses at the present time, and most of them are involved in research rather than private practice. Hopefully, more and more doctors will undertake this task in the future. However, as Dr. Shettles repeatedly points out, sperm analysis is rarely worth the trouble and expense, since his studies show that most individuals, including those who have children of mostly one sex, are capable of begetting the other sex—simply by following the home procedures outlined in this book. The fact that a couple has children all of one sex is far more likely to be a consequence of bad luck than of genetics. Only in cases in which the husband's brothers, father, grandfather, and other relatives have consistently produced children of the same sex is it highly likely that there is a genetic factor at work. And when a man fathers nothing but girls, this might be a result of neither bad luck nor genetics, but a low sperm count, a condition that can be partially remedied by abstinence from intercourse, as suggested in the preceding chapter.

Q: "We want a girl. What color should the Tes-Tape be at the time of intercourse?"

A: Again, each woman will have to determine this for herself by daily testing, preferably through three or four complete cycles. The idea is to recognize the color that the tape is two and three days prior to the time at which it reaches its darkest stage (ovulation time). The color will vary from woman to woman.

Q: "I'm presently on the birth-control pill. How long should I wait after going off it before trying to choose the sex of my next baby?"

A: Most doctors say four to six months. Use these months to refamiliarize yourself with your cycle and to determine the exact time of ovulation each month.

Q: "Can the douche harm the offspring in any way?"

A: Dr. Shettles says there is no danger whatever, to the mother or the offspring. All babies born using these techniques have been completely normal.

Q: "I read in a newspaper that the acid kills the male sperm and the alkali kills the female sperm. Is this right?"

A: Some newspaper reports on Dr. Shettles' findings were misleading. The alkaline douche favors both types of sperm, but shows the male-producing sperm cells off in their best light, letting them use to full advantage the one thing they have over the gynosperms: speed. The acid slows down both types but affects the gynosperms least, because they are larger and have greater resistance.

Q: "I would like to use Dr. Shettles' sex-selection techniques but, as a Catholic, I am wondering if they run contrary to Church doctrine?"

A: As we shall see in the next chapter, the Catholic Church does not object to the procedures.

Q: "Is there a way to separate the two types of sperm, so that we would have a 100 percent chance of success? I am willing to undergo artificial insemination if there is any way to do this."

A: A number of exciting separation techniques are in the works or have been proposed; some have already been used successfully in animal studies. These techniques and the ways in which they will probably be applied to humans are discussed in Part Two of this book: "Sex in the Future."

Q: "My periods are very irregular, and my temperature varies so little that I can't determine when I ovulate. I want a little girl. Would it hurt me to douche with vinegar solution every day during the period when I think I'm fertile?"

A: Repeated douching is not harmful. However, in cases in which temperature or periods seem very irregular, the Tes-Tape or fertility kit should be used to determine time of ovulation. And remember that at the time of ovulation a vinegar douche may not be enough to keep the androsperms from getting through.

Q: "How long does it take the sperm to get to the egg, assuming it is already waiting in the Fallopian tube?"

A: Generally about an hour.

Q: "What time of day should the Tes-Tape be used?"

A: Actually, it is best to use it twice a day, once in the morning and once in the evening. It should always be used before intercourse and, of course, before any sort of douche.

Q: "Who makes the 'fertility test kit' and what is it actually called?"

A: It is called the Fertility Test Kit—A Home Method for Detection of Ovulation, manufactured by Weston Laboratories of Ottawa, Illinois. This kit contains a cigar-shaped applicator, as well as the tape itself.

Q: "People like us have read about the sex-selection procedure with interest and, especially, envy. By 'people like us,' I mean those who can't seem to have any children at all. Does any of this new research offer us any hope?"

A: There is a new technique that promises considerable hope for the infertile. It is a procedure that may enable some of those who have been considered "completely infertile" or "irreversibly infertile" to have children—and select their sex at the same time. This is discussed in Part Two.

Q: "My wife claims to have read or heard some place that the type of shorts a man wears can affect his fertility. If she weren't a nurse I'd say she was crazy. Is there any truth in this idea and, if so, could it have anything to do with the sex of a man's children?"

A: The wife's claims are accurate. Dr. John Rock of Harvard, one of the developers of the birth-control pill, states: "Any clothing that prevents maintenance of an intrascrotal temperature that is at least 1 degree Centigrade below body temperature will significantly lower sperm output. Daily wear of a well-fitting, closely knit jockstrap results in infertility after four weeks. . . . Normal output gradually is resumed after another three weeks without such interference. Enclosing the scrotum in ice for one-half hour daily may increase sperm output in perhaps 10 percent of moderately oligospermic (low-sperm-count) men and result in a long-awaited pregnancy."

Dr. Shettles, commenting on this, notes again that low sperm count is associated with a predominance of female offspring. So it would appear that a man can increase his chances of producing boys not only by abstaining from intercourse before ovulation but by shying away from all tight-fitting, well-insulated underwear. The ice is optional.

Q: "Can the sort of occupation or environment that a person works in have any effect on the sex of his offspring?"

A: There is only sketchy information available on this. Physique, emotional factors, diet, and environment could all have some influence on acidity and alkalinity within the body and this, in turn, could conceivably have some effect on sex of offspring. Frogmen are reported to produce an unusually high number of girls; individuals living at high altitudes tend to be infertile and, probably as a result of low sperm counts, produce more girls than boys. Heat, as we have just seen, can also result in low sperm count, when it acts to raise the temperature within the scrotum.

Q: "As one who is professionally involved in family planning, I have mixed feelings about our new ability to choose sex. On the one hand, it will help people limit the size of their families by getting the desired sex right at the start. But what if there is some fad that makes boys more popular than girls, or vice versa? We could end up with a terrible imbalance."

A: This question, along with other sociological implications of sex selection, is taken up in the next chapter.

5

What if Everyone Wants Boys? *Some Sociological Considerations*

History indicates that a desire for sons is almost universal. The Romans had to pay a fourth of an *as* in taxes for every girl child born to them, but only a sixth of an *as* for every boy. Moses ruled that a woman is "unclean" for a full fourteen days following the birth of a girl but for only a week following the birth of a boy. The Jewish Talmud declares that "when a girl is born, the walls are crying," and the *Holy Book of Islam* observes that "when an Arab hears that a daughter has been born to him, his face becomes saddened." Among the Conibos of South America, a husband traditionally responds to the birth of a girl by spitting on his wife's bed. Even today, in many kingdoms, the birth of a prince is announced with two or three times more cannon blasts than a princess gets.

All of this has led some observers to believe that our new ability to choose the sex of our children will result in a bumper crop of boys—with various unpleasant consequences. There is no way to prove that this will be true, but it is worth discussing—along with some of the other pros and cons of sex selection.

One man who is concerned about some of the possible results of sex selection is Dr. Amitai Etzioni, a professor of sociology at Columbia University. In an article published recently in a scientific journal,* he addressed himself to the probability that a great many parents will be taking advantage of sex-selection methods "five years from now or sooner." Then he cited studies showing that the demand for male children is 55 to 65 percent greater than for females. In light of this, he fears "an overproduction of boys" and predicts that this "will very likely affect most aspects of social life." He goes so far as to say that parental control over sex of offspring could bring to an end the two-party political system and throw the country back into a frontier atmosphere.

This may not be as farfetched as it sounds, provided Dr. Etzioni's basic premise—that parents will consistently overproduce males, given the chance—is correct. Before returning to that, listen to what Dr. Etzioni has to say: he notes that men vote "systematically and significantly more Democratic than women." Since the Republican Party has been steadily losing support over the last gen-

---

* Dr. Amitai Etzioni, "Sex Control, Science, and Society," *Science*, 161 (Sept. 13, 1968), pp. 1107–12.

eration, according to the professor, he believes that "another five-point loss could undermine the two-party system to a point where Democratic control would be uninterrupted."

First of all, it is safe to say that Dr. Etzioni does not believe that sex selection is a Democratic Party plot. His theory is certainly an intriguing one, but it seems difficult to believe that if the Republican Party should fall by the way it would be simply because of an overproduction of males. No one can say for sure what the political orientation of future male generations will be. Then, too, many of Dr. Etzioni's colleagues have said that women are becoming more and more the dominant sex, while men are receding more and more into the background and even taking up household duties. Perhaps in the future, the activist woman will associate almost exclusively with the labor-oriented Democratic Party, while the domesticated male will take up residence in the Republican Party. Or suppose that the two-party system should temporarily collapse as a result of heightened male supremacy. Men have about as many disagreements as women and can be counted on to go their separate ways—via new political parties—at some point in the future. Finally, many studies indicate that party ties are coming to mean less and less to voters; issues and personalities play an ever greater role in politics, which may be one reason that, as of this writing, we have a Republican president despite the great numerical superiority of registered Democrats.

Dr. Etzioni goes on to point out that women, as churchgoers, consumers of culture, and so on, do more than men to maintain what is generally known as "civilization." Hence, he concludes that "a significant and cumulative male surplus will . . . produce a society with some of the rougher features of a frontier town." This new frontier, he predicts, will be populated by a lot of single men on the make (sort of latter-day saddle bums, gunslingers, and cowpokes) for the few available females. To take up the slack, he goes on, prostitution and homosexuality will increase substantially. Further, he foresees an increase in interracial and interclass tensions. Minority groups and the lower classes put a higher premium on male offspring than do the more affluent, and these groups in particular, Dr. Etzioni believes, could be counted on to use sex-selection procedures. This bumper crop of lower-class boys, he says, would then be forced to seek out girls from higher status groups, thus increasing class and race strife.

There is one major chink in Dr. Etzioni's reasoning. The lower classes, with illiteracy problems, deep-seated suspicion and fear of anything that "interferes" with basic, biological functions, and susceptibility to superstition and folk medicine, will, unfortunately, be the last to take advantage of sex selection on any significant scale. Birth-control pills, for example, could be of greatest benefit to the poor. Yet it is the more affluent and the more sophisticated who are the greatest consumers of birth-control devices and chemicals. The poor spurn them or

simply don't know about them, partly because of fear
and suspicion, partly because of economic and educa-
tional factors. Many women I talked to in depressed areas
of Appalachia and the Mississippi Delta had never even
heard of the birth-control pill. Such women are hardly
prepared to plan the *number* of children they have, let
alone their sexes.

Commentators other than Dr. Etzioni have added
other fears to the list, fears once again based on the
notion that sex-selection techniques will help fuel boy-
girl fads that will have "disastrous" consequences. If
female offspring should become the rage, they say, society will have to give its blessings to polygamy; if boys
should become the vogue, then polyandry would have to
prevail. "The dangers are not apocalyptic," Dr. Etzioni
concedes, "but are they worth the gains to be made?"

Hopefully, the preceding paragraphs have demonstrated that the "dangers" have been somewhat exagger-
ated, even if one accepts Dr. Etzioni's basic premise—that
parents will overproduce one sex. If that premise is un-
true, of course, then the alleged dangers completely dis-
solve. Again, only time will tell the story, but Dr. Shettles is personally convinced that parents will not use his
techniques to produce mostly males rather than females,
or vice versa.

"Over the years, parents have expressed only one desire," he says, "and that is to have families that are well
balanced in terms of sex. Most find an equal number of
boys and girls ideal." The same attitude emerges from

the hundreds of letters that arrived following early pub-
licity of Dr. Shettles' work: families with three boys, for
example, wanted nothing so much as a girl, while those
with a preponderance of girls were equally enthusiastic
about being able to beget boys.

Many couples said they had initially planned for a
family of two children, hoping for one of each. But when
both offspring turned out to be of the same sex they made
a third attempt and so on. "We now have four boys,"
one woman wrote, "and that is two more than we really
wanted. If we had known of this research several years
ago we would never have ended up in this situation. Of
course, we love our sons and have only ourselves to blame.
But we just kept thinking: once more and this time it
will have to be a girl." So it is not too farfetched to
envision sex selection making a significant contribution
in the effort to control the population explosion. How
much better it would be to achieve the ideal family balance in two tries instead of three or four or more, or
never.

In any event, it seems, to return for a moment to Dr.
Etzioni, that overproduction of one sex, if such should
occur, would ultimately create a reaction that would
cause parents to start producing the other sex again. As
soon as something useful, whether it be beefsteak or
females, is in short supply, there is almost always a huge
demand for it, followed by a massive effort to produce
the desired commodity in volume sufficient to meet that
demand.

G. Rattray Taylor, in his book *The Biological Time-Bomb,* takes an optimistic point of view about this: "It may be," he writes, "that in Western societies there would be some slight preference for a son, expressed perhaps as a tendency on the part of some people to have sons only, more often than daughters only. I suspect that this tendency would not be so marked that it could not be checked by propaganda and good sense."

The "dangers" of sex selection are at this point nothing more than vague speculations. The advantages of sex selection, on the other hand, are manifest: parental satisfaction, balanced families, very possibly smaller families and, as we are about to see, *healthier* families.

Where does health come in? Sometimes health—or lack of it—is attached to our sex chromosomes. Only males, for example, suffer from hemophilia, the grim and often fatal "bleeder's disease" that is not so rare as many people think. Similar hereditary, "sex-linked" diseases include one type of muscular dystrophy and numerous enzyme-deficiency disorders that can kill, cripple, and retard for life.

Though most of these diseases remain incurable, they can be prevented. Take hemophilia, for example, often called the "disease of kings," because it afflicted so many men in reigning European families. This disease leaves its victims very nearly defenseless against even small cuts and wounds because the blood in these individuals lacks the factor that enables it to clot effectively. The recessive gene that determines whether a person will suffer from this disease is carried, when it exists at all, in one of the two X chromosomes of each immature female sex cell. After final cell division, only half of these cells carry the recessive gene. If one of these carrier eggs is mated with an X-bearing (female-producing) sperm, the female offspring will not suffer from the disease because the normal gene, inherited from the father, is dominant. If, however, the carrier egg is fertilized by a Y-bearing sperm, the disease will manifest itself because the Y chromosome does not carry the gene. Doctors can now tell women who are known carriers of hemophilia that their offspring, if male, will have a 50–50 chance of suffering from the disease.

Many women who discover that they are carriers of sex-linked diseases, such as hemophilia, try to get abortions when they learn that they are going to give birth to male offspring. (The sex of an unborn child can now be determined three or four months into pregnancy.) Such abortions could be avoided altogether if these carriers of sex-linked diseases could simply avoid conceiving children of the vulnerable sex.

The value of sex selection in helping to overcome these diseases motivates many researchers in this field, such as Drs. Robert Edwards and Richard Gardner of Cambridge University. Writing in *New Scientist,* they point out that "the elimination of these disorders in one generation, by a judicious choice of the sex of the offspring, would not only be of direct benefit to that generation, but would benefit the race for generations to come." More on Edwards and Gardner in Part Two: "Sex in the Future."

What other advantages might accrue from our ability to choose the sex of our children? One medical man, Dr. A. L. Benedict, has suggested that sex selection might have some psychological benefits beyond the obvious ones that come from having sexually balanced families. Some parents, Dr. Benedict believes, are really suited to raising children of only one sex. It may be that a woman who has a strong aversion to little girls is mentally disturbed and shouldn't really have *any* children. But since she is likely to go ahead no matter what we think, isn't it better if she has nothing but boys—better for her children as well as herself? Similarly, there are men who have such a strong desire to beget children of one sex that their offspring, should they turn out to be of the "wrong" gender, suffer for it. The father's disappointment is quickly communicated to the child, very often without words ever being spoken; as many a psychiatric case history has shown, the child may feel at once rejected and guilty—guilty for having "failed" to be born a member of the opposite sex. The child may then either withdraw into himself or perhaps try to correct his error by acting as though he were indeed a member of the opposite sex. If the situation continues to deteriorate in this way, the child may be psychologically scarred for life, unable to function properly in his biologically assigned sexual role.

Beyond this, sex selection could come in handy in a number of situations in which, for some reason, there exists a particular shortage of one sex or the other. In the days of the woman-scarce Old West, for example, it is probable that there was a big demand for female offspring, at least in the towns where single men congregated on weekends. On the frontier farms, of course, it would have been likely that boys would prevail, since they could be expected to help with the heavy work. As we move out into the new frontier of space it is likely that certain circumstances and environments will again call for the proliferation of one sex or the other—and this time the means to meet the demand will be at hand. We will be similarly prepared if war or disease should destroy a great many men or women. Perhaps in the future, governments will call upon their constituents to fulfill their patriotic duties, not so much by paying their taxes as by producing boys or girls, whichever happens to be needed as a result of some catastrophe.

For the moment we can content ourselves with the fact that a method of sex selection has been developed and is at our disposal. For the first time in all time, parents have the opportunity to make a scientific attempt at choosing the sex of their children and to make that attempt with a justifiably high expectation of success. The procedures involved are safe and simple, and nothing about them is morally or ethically objectionable. Protestant ministers have inquired about the procedures with the intention of incorporating them into their own family planning, rabbis have cooperated with Dr. Shettles in his research, and the Roman Catholic Church has be-

stowed its blessing. Monsignor Hugh Curran, director of
the family-life bureau of the Archdiocese of New York,
says that the Church has no objections to Dr. Shettles'
sex-selection procedures "as long as the intent of these
efforts is not to prevent conception."

part II

SEX IN THE FUTURE

6

Sex Selection in the Future:
The Test-Tube Generation

In Part One, a procedure for sex selection that can
be used now was examined in detail. The procedure requires a little work and patience on the part of parents
and, although results have been impressive, it does not
provide a 100 percent guarantee of success. This opening
chapter of Part Two discusses some of the ways scientists
expect to achieve even easier and more foolproof means
of sex selection in the future. Some of these procedures
will sound more like science fiction than science fact
(though most are in the works right now). Some may
seem to you more like horrors than wonders, but bear
in mind that everything new takes some getting used to.

The least sensational prospects for the future of sex
selection, and these are dazzling enough, are based on
Dr. Shettles' discovery that sperms come in two distinct
sizes, the larger, oval-shaped type producing females and

the smaller, rounder ones producing males. Several researchers reasoned that if two such populations really exist, then there should be some way to separate them and use them, via artificial insemination, to guarantee birth of the desired sex.

Early experiments with animal sperm yielded only partial success. The Soviets, for example, tried to separate the two types of sperm by using electrical techniques called "electrophoresis." The idea was that the two varieties might have different electrical charges and could thus be segregated like protons and electrons. Results were inconclusive, and researchers next turned to centrifugation techniques that exploit the difference in mass between the two types of sperm. The centrifuge spins the sperm cells until the two types become stratified, each type falling into its own zone according to mass. Swedish scientists were the first to have any success with this, achieving the birth of eleven male calves in a row by using sperm of lesser mass.

More recently, a Michigan State University researcher, Dr. Manuel Gordon, has returned to the electrophoresis method of sperm separation and has had better results than the Soviets. Dr. Gordon put rabbit sperm in a mild saline solution and then passed a weak electrical current through it. The male-producing sperms tended to migrate toward the negative electrical pole, while the female type headed for the positive pole. Inseminating rabbits with cells from the negative pole, Dr. Gordon produced males 64 percent of the time; using the sperms that migrated to the positive pole, he got females 71 percent of the time. These results are not yet good enough to guarantee even rabbits the desired sex 100 percent of the time, but they are certainly encouraging enough so that research in electrophoresis is not likely to be abandoned.

Better results have been obtained by using yet a third method of separating the two types: sedimentation. Work in this field started when Dr. B. C. Bhattacharya, an Indian zoologist, noticed that peasants in his country preferred to bring their cows in for artificial insemination at sundown rather than earlier in the day, claiming that this resulted in more bull calves. Dr. Bhattacharya checked into this and found that it was true: cattle inseminated later in the day *did* produce more male offspring. Looking for a scientific explanation, he concluded that the two types of sperm drifted to the bottom of storage containers at different rates, the heavier female-producing variety reaching the bottom first. By the end of the day, he reasoned, far more of the lighter, male-producing sperm would be left at the top of the containers, which would explain why more bull calves were conceived at sundown.

Moving on to the famed Max Planck Institute for Animal Breeding at Hagen, West Germany, Dr. Bhattacharya undertook a series of experiments with rabbits, inseminating thousands of does with sperm that had settled under a variety of conditions. At first he got mixed results but then finally hit upon a formula that made "sedimentation," as he called his technique, look promising indeed.

The trick was to refrigerate the sperm (mixed in a protective solution of egg yolk and glycerol) for about twelve hours at a point just about the freezing mark. This prevented the sperms from swimming about, and, in their immobile state, they separated far more readily than they had previously. Dr. Bhattacharya used the refrigerated samples to impregnate 176 rabbits. Those inseminated with sperms that had settled to the bottom of the containers produced 72 percent females. The rabbits that were impregnated with cells from the top of the samples gave birth to males 78 percent of the time. Encouraged by this, Dr. Bhattacharya is hopeful that the technique can be refined to the point that the two types of sperm can be completely segregated. Before too long, it may become routine for prospective fathers to leave samples of sperm with their doctors to be "sedimented" and separated preparatory to artificial insemination of their wives. When the doctor asks, "Top or bottom?" he'll really mean, "Boy or girl?"

An even more exciting prospect is envisioned by Dr. E. James Leiberman of the National Institutes of Health in Washington, D.C. He suggests that the modern woman will eventually have at her disposal "a special diaphragm that will let through only the sperm that carries, let's say, the male sex and hold back those that carry the female sex." Selecting sex, then, would become a mere matter of which diaphragm a woman chooses to wear.

Dr. Charles Birch, head of the Sydney (Australia) University School of Biological Sciences, goes one-up on Dr. Leiberman, predicting that science will one day come up with a pill to determine sex. If male offspring are desired, Dr. Birch says, the husband will take one of the "little boy pills" just before intercourse or, if a female is wanted, a "little girl pill." When one stops to consider how effective such commonplace chemicals as vinegar and baking soda can be, Dr. Birch's prediction doesn't really seem so utopian after all. Nor does it seem unreasonable to expect that such a pill will become available within the next two or three decades.

Even if all of these methods fail to achieve the ideal (that is, the desired sex every time), there is yet another approach to sex selection that leaves no opening whatever for failure. It is far more controversial than the techniques discussed so far, for reasons that will become apparent. Cambridge University physiologists Richard Gardner and Robert Edwards are the scientists involved. They mated rabbits, then removed the embryos before they had become attached to the lining of the mothers' wombs. Then, using microsurgical tools, they removed from each embryo a few hundred cells, which they examined under the microscope for the presence of sex chromatin, found only in female cells. In this way they could separate the tiny embryos into boys and girls at the very earliest stage of their development.

After letting the embryos recover from the microsurgery, by bathing them in a culture medium for several

hours, the scientists implanted them in slits they had
made in the wombs of the mature female rabbits. The
embryos developed naturally, and, *in every case*, turned
out at birth to be the sex that the researchers predicted
they would be. Of course, if a woman wanted to control
the sex of her offspring in this way, she might have to
have more than one embryo to choose from at the beginning. Even this is possible, since there are drugs that
can induce "superovulation," or the release of many eggs
at once, instead of the normal one per month. Then,
when all of these eggs are fertilized, but before they have
attached themselves to the lining of the uterus, they could
be washed out of the Fallopian tubes and "sexed" under
the microscope. That is, they could be separated into
males and females in the same fashion that the rabbit
embryos were. Then, if a boy is desired, one of the males
could be implanted in the uterus and the rest of the
embryos discarded.

It is this discarding, this "jettisoning of test-tube babies," that invites controversy. The British journal *New
Scientist* has some doubts about the moral and ethical
aspects of the procedure: "Dr. Edwards' plan takes no
account of those 'bench' embryos not selected for survival. Would their destruction by the laboratory at-
tendant who cleaned up after a day's work amount to an
act of abortion?" This depends on the point at which
society says life begins. Currently, the Catholic Church
maintains that life commences at the moment of conception—when sperm and egg merge in the Fallopian

tube. There is some chance, however, that this "definition" may be modified; a number of prominent scientists, including Dr. A. S. Parkes, believe that nidation—the point at which the embryo attaches itself to the lining of the womb—should mark the real beginning of life, since it is only at this point that the embryo really begins to develop. If this viewpoint ultimately prevails, there can be no objections to the Edwards approach, which guarantees the sex you want every time.

It is worth noting, in passing, that some interesting side benefits could accrue from these egg-implanting techniques. Experimental biologists have already demonstrated that it is possible to remove eggs from one animal, inseminate them, and then implant them in yet other animals. Cattle breeders are profitably using this technique in many areas of the United States right now. Prize cows are chemically induced to superovulate, sometimes giving up as many as a hundred eggs at a time. These are removed, fertilized with the sperm of prize bulls, and then implanted in the wombs of lesser cows, which carry the babies to term as if they were their own. The real mother, meanwhile, is free to gambol about the pasture, unencumbered by pregnancy. All she has to do is produce more prize eggs.

One biologist, Dr. E. S. E. Hafez of Washington State University, notes that egg implantation, besides offering a means of controlling sex (as in Dr. Edwards' work), could help many women who were previously unable to have children to become pregnant for the first time. A

great deal of infertility among women is caused by mal-
formation or blockage of the Fallopian tubes. These
women produce viable eggs each month, but sperm cells
are unable to reach them. Dr. Hafez predicts that within
a few years doctors will be able to remove these eggs,
fertilize them with the husband's sperm in a test tube,
and then implant them in the wife's womb at the appropriate moment. Similarly, Dr. Hafez points out,
women who do not ovulate at all may still be able to experience pregnancy and childbirth, rather than submit to
the uncertainties of adoption. These women would simply have the eggs of other women (fertilized by their own
husbands' sperm) implanted in their wombs. The donors
of the eggs, it seems likely, will be anonymous, just as
sperm donors in artificial insemination are today—and the
woman will carry the child to term and give birth to it
just as if it were her own.

In addition, the woman who produces viable eggs but
is unable to bear a child because of heart disease or some
other condition that might be severely aggravated by
pregnancy could have her fertilized egg implanted in another woman—perhaps a sister—who would carry it to
term and then relinquish it to its real mother. Some
scientists have even suggested that the wealthy woman or
the career woman who wants children but doesn't want
to take time out for pregnancy might *hire* another woman
to undergo implantation and carry the baby to birth for
her. Just what would happen if the mother surrogate re-
fused to give up the child at birth remains to be seen.

Probably the most stunning means of sex selection for the future is a procedure called cloning, which has mind-stretching implications far beyond mere selection of sex. The word "cloning" comes from a Greek word meaning "cutting" and describes a means of reproduction that by-passes sexual intercourse. Cloning makes it possible not only to choose sex but to produce genetically identical "copies" of prize bulls, race horses, Olympic-caliber athletes, war heroes, great philosophers, leading scientists, even rock musicians such as the Beatles by the tens, hundreds, or thousands, whatever society needs or demands. And each will be a precise duplicate, a genetic carbon copy of the original. In addition, cloning will make it possible for a woman to bear a child without the hitherto necessary union of egg and sperm. More astonishing, it will also make possible the birth of a child whose only parent is a male. All clonal offspring have only one real parent and will grow up to be the identical twin of that parent.

To understand this fantastic state of affairs, it is necessary to review a little basic biology. First of all, remember that there are two general kinds of cells: body cells, each of which has a nucleus containing forty-six chromosomes, and sex cells (the sperm and egg), each of which has only half as many, or twenty-three, chromosomes. That's why two sex cells have to get together to make a new individual; one half of the chromosomes come from the mother and one half from the father. Remember, too, that the human egg looks something like a chicken's egg, consisting of a yolklike nucleus and a surrounding, clear fluid called the cytoplasm. The cytoplasm contributes nothing to the genetic makeup of an individual, since the genes are all inside the nucleus. The job of the cytoplasm is mainly to protect and nourish the nucleus and its payload of chromosomes and genes.

In recent years, however, scientists have discovered an important additional function of the cytoplasm: it seems to act as a control center that tells the nucleus when to "switch on" and start dividing to create new life. As long as the egg nucleus just sits there with only twenty-three chromosomes, the cytoplasm does nothing. But as soon as the sperm swims through and fertilizes the egg, the cytoplasm is chemically "programmed" to send a message to the nucleus that says, in effect: "You are now a fertilized egg cell, complete with forty-six chromosomes, and as such you must start dividing at once." Which is precisely what happens. The "switched-on" cell takes off, dividing billions of times to create a whole new person.

All of those billions of body cells, in any given individual, have a common ancestry: the single, fertilized egg cell. They all contain an identical set of chromosomes. Yet unlike the fertilized egg cell, the body cells have limited and very specialized creative capabilities. Some make only teeth, others form liver cells, and still others go into making up hair. And so on. Each body cell has the full number of chromosomes and all the genetic blueprints necessary to create a whole new individual, but most of their components are "switched off." The genes and nucleotides in the forty-six chromosomes of a skin cell, for example, are all turned off except for those few that go into making skin. So in this sense, most of the cell is "wasted."

For years, scientists have been fascinated with the idea of taking a body cell and switching it on so that it would start dividing and create a replica of the individual from which it came. No sexual union would be necessary in this sort of reproduction, they reasoned, since all forty-six chromosomes would be present in the single cell at the outset. Incredible as the whole thing seemed, nobody could think of any valid objections to it, but neither could anybody think of a way to bring this feat off, even in the lowliest forms of life.

Nobody, that is, until Dr. F. C. Steward of Cornell University scored the long-awaited breakthrough a few years ago. His experiments were with nothing more exalted than carrots, but the results of his work electrified the scientific world. Dr. Steward scraped an unfertilized cell from the body of a carrot and placed it in a specially prepared nutrient bath that contained, among other things, coconut milk. In this solution, the cell began dividing as if it "thought" it had been pollinated. As Dr. Steward put it, "It was as if the coconut milk had acted like a clutch putting the cell's idling engine of growth into gear." From a single body cell, the Cornell team got a mature carrot that was the genetic twin of the carrot that donated that cell. "We were hardly prepared," Dr. Steward reported, "for such dramatic results."

Now Dr. J. B. Gurdon of Oxford University has devised an ingenious method of duplicating this feat in the animal kingdom. Building on the pioneering work of Drs. R. Briggs and T. J. King, two American scientists, Dr. Gurdon uses the following technique to achieve asexual reproduction in the African clawed frog: first he takes an unfertilized egg cell from a frog and destroys its nucleus with ultraviolet radiation. Then he takes a body cell from another frog (often scraping it from a remote spot such as the intestinal wall) and removes its nucleus with the help of a microscope and tiny surgical tools. Next, he implants the body-cell nucleus into the egg cell, the original nucleus of which had only half as many chromosomes.

In this way the control center in the egg-cell cytoplasm is "tricked" into thinking that fertilization has taken place—because suddenly there is a full set of chromosomes in its nucleus. Thus, a body-cell nucleus, previously nothing more than a lowly speck of intestine, is switched on to divide and produce a spanking new tadpole. And that tadpole grows up to be an identical twin of the body-cell donor. To demonstrate that the new frog is the "offspring" of just one parent and that the parent is the body-cell donor and not the egg-cell donor, Dr. Gurdon uses frogs of clearly distinctive types as the two donors in each case. Invariably, the new frog is the exact image of the body-cell donor. The egg-cell cytoplasm is merely the nutrient material that it feeds on in its formative stage.

When and how will this procedure be applied to the human animal? According to Nobel-Prize-winning geneticist Joshua Lederberg, "There is nothing to suggest any particular difficulty about accomplishing this in mammals or man, though it will rightly be admired as a technical tour de force when it is first accomplished." Like Kimball Atwood, a professor of microbiology at the University of Illinois, he believes this could occur within the next few years, though it is unlikely that it would be used on any significant scale for several decades. Society will almost certainly use cloning in animal breeding before that, but the idea of cloning people will take some getting used to. As for the *how* of cloning people, that's easier to speculate on. It will be done in the same way that Dr. Gurdon clones his frogs, except that in this case the surgically manipulated eggs will have to be implanted in the womb for development. Here again, even though a woman must furnish the egg-cell cytoplasm and the uterine environment for normal development of the fetus, the child that results can still be the offspring of a man—and of a man alone.

Imagine a couple in the year 2000 deciding it is time for another baby. Population problems being what they are, they must first apply for a license to have a child. If the license is granted, they receive a prescription from the appropriate medical authority for a drug that acts as a temporary antidote to the infertility agent that is regularly dumped into the municipal water supply. Then the couple has a number of options open to them. They can take a chance and have a baby "in the old way," simply by having intercourse without any sort of "interference." Or they can use the douche and timing procedures developed by Dr. Shettles in the 1960's, thus greatly increasing their chances of having offspring of the sex they desire. Or, if they don't mind utilizing artificial insemination, they can be *guaranteed* the sex of their choice by using the "sexing" techniques that Dr. Edwards began applying to humans in the 1970's. Then, there's the diaphragm of the 1980's that lets through sperm cells of only one type. Possibly by this time they may even have access to the pill that determines sex; then if they want a boy, the husband will simply take a blue pill a few hours before intercourse. Or he'll take a pink pill if they want a girl.

Or they could opt for the newest and most exotic technique of all—one that would completely bypass the sexual union of sperm and egg and offer something more than a mere guarantee that the offspring will be of the sex desired. This, of course, is the cloning technique (which will probably require a special license, above and beyond that required for more conventional childbirth). Suppose the couple wants a boy by clonal reproduction. The husband will then go to his doctor and have several cells removed from his arm. These will be examined under the microscope, and a particularly healthy-looking one will be picked out. The doctor will remove the cell's nucleus very carefully, hold it up to the light, and say, "Congratulations, here's your baby boy." Then he will remove one of the wife's egg cells, vaporize its nucleus with radiation from a laser, and insert the body-cell nucleus in its place. Finally, he will implant this doctored cell in the wife's uterus (much as Dr. Edwards already implants animal embryos) and then let Nature take her course.

Nine months later, a baby boy will arrive, and everyone will have to agree that it is *literally* "a chip off the old block." Microscopic studies will show that it is genetically identical to its "father" in every detail, that it is really more an identical twin (that arrived several years late) than a son. As the child grows up, of course, it will look exactly like its father, which ought to satisfy even the vainest of men. If a girl were wanted, the body-cell nucleus would come from the wife's arm or hand. And would then be used to "fertilize" her own egg cell, making parthenogenesis, or "virgin birth," a reality!

It is probably evident to the reader that cloning could have applications that reach far beyond the control of sex. The world-famed biologist J. B. S. Haldane was one of the first to recognize the possibilities. He proposed that geniuses and others who had made extraordinary contributions to society be cloned. During their retirement, he said, they could teach their clonal offspring all they knew. (Since teacher and student, in this situation, would be so much alike right down—or up—to the tiniest brain cell, the "generation gap" that plagues contemporary education would probably be nonexistent.) Individuals valued for their physical abilities, such as dancers, athletes, soldiers, or astronauts, should be cloned young, Dr. Haldane said, so that they would have all the vigor necessary to train their replicas. He proposed, too, that some considerable effort should be given to seeking out and cloning lesser-known individuals who possess what he called "special effects," such as lack of the pain sense, night vision, resistance to radiation, inability to hear high-pitched sounds (which might be used in weapons of the future), dwarfism (which could come in handy in the high gravitational fields that we will encounter as we explore some of the other planets), and so on.

7

Male and Female:
Will There Still
Be a Difference?

Traditionally, society has been unbending in its insistence that man is man and woman is woman, and never the twain shall meet. Any deviation from this standard is generally received with horror and indignation. In Basel, Switzerland, in 1474 a chicken cock was, in the words of geneticist F. A. E. Crew, "burned at the stake for the unnatural crime of laying an egg." This affront to 15th-century sensibilities was nothing short of a "perversion of the devil." Nobody even stopped to consider that there might be some physiological explanation for the phenomenon. After all, everybody *knew* cocks were supposed to strut and crow, hens were supposed to lay the eggs—period.

Today, parents still remain fearfully on the watch for any sign that a son's behavior or attitudes may not be "all boy," or that a daughter may not be "all girl." Overt homosexuality is regarded by most parents as more catastrophic than death or taxes. Yet, as the heroes of today's folk-rock culture keep informing us, "the times they are a-changin'."

When it comes to sex, the times are changing on two separate but parallel fronts. One can be called "the New Biology," the other "the New Morality." These two are in concert in questioning society's rigid conception of "maleness" and "femaleness." And, in a very limited time, the New Biology and the New Morality have been so successful in revealing the errors of this conception that one cannot avoid wondering whether the day will come—in a utopian or nightmarish world of the future, depending on how you look at it—when there will cease to be any practical difference, biological or sociological, between men and women.

It is not inconceivable that the New Biology will one day, however distant, enable man to change sex at will or even to possess both sexes in one body, rendering obsolete the sort of sex selection we have been discussing in this book. With something as astonishing as cloning *already* within our grasp, who can doubt that far more amazing things lie ahead? And when we ask whether these sometimes frightening new abilities will actually be used, we come back to the New Morality.

The New Morality is largely a commodity of the cult-of-youth that is upon us today and promises to engulf us tomorrow, as the tide of people "under thirty" overrides the old—and older—majority. Enemies of the New Morality declare that it is nothing but a high-flung name for chaos, a cover for those who seek to destroy the institutions of family, home, manhood, and mother-hood, a haven for irresponsible hedonists and perverts bent on personal gratification without regard for any-thing or anyone else. Disciples of the New Morality reject this characterization wholesale, insisting that theirs is a morality dedicated to the liberation of the human spirit, mind, and body; to the "actualization" of the human potential to love and be loved without the twin hangups of hypocrisy and guilt, which they say character-ize the Old Morality and its Puritan ethic.

Though the rhetoric of both sides is fraught with hyperbole, certain things cannot be denied. The New Morality *has* unquestionably contributed to a new per-missiveness which, in turn, has revealed that both men and women are less than satisfied with the rigid roles society has assigned them. There is controversy over whether homosexuality is really increasing as rapidly as some people say, but nobody questions the fact that it is becoming ever more overt. Homosexuals—particularly the younger ones who adhere to the honesty-without-shame ethic—defiantly announce that they have nothing to hide. Many city dwellers are presently so accustomed to the sight of two boys or two girls (many of them looking a lot like the kids next door) walking down the street hand-in-hand that they scarcely bat an eye anymore. At the same time the mass-circulation magazines are regal-

ing us with the details of "group sex," in which bisexuality (or, as *Esquire* Magazine put it recently, "the
ability to swing both ways") frequently prevails.

And no wonder, some of you may be thinking, since
it's often difficult to tell the boys from the girls anyhow,
with the new hair styles and the trend toward "unisex"
clothing that is identical for both sexes. As this is being
written, leading clothes designers for men are sending
their male models before the public shamelessly decked
out in earrings, necklaces, bracelets—and equipped with
purses! *Time* Magazine recently ran a series of pictures
of prominent men, many of them married, who have
rushed to keep up with the times and can now be seen
toting handbags and purses. Earrings have been slower
to catch on, for what little comfort that may offer.

Meanwhile, sociologists continue to dig up data showing
that the sexes are not only becoming more and more alike
but that, in some cases, they are actually switching roles.
Women, they point out, are abandoning the home and
taking to the office and even the workshop at an ever-
increasing pace; men are finding that they no longer
have to be so aggressive about "wearing the pants" and can
actually look the neighbors in the face without being
laughed at if they stay home and watch the kids while
the wife works. Then there is the sudden (and, to some,
ominous) emergence of "feminist" and "women's liberation" movements. And perhaps because women are becoming aware of the fact that they constitute the stronger
and more resistant sex and because of the idea (perhaps

soon to be established as fact) that they are capable of more intense sexual drives and orgasms than men, they are becoming steadily more assertive in courtship and seduction. The male-produced propaganda that females should be the passive partner in sex is rapidly being discredited, and women are saying, "What have we been missing? Let's get moving!"

In his book *The Second Genesis*, Albert Rosenfeld, the science editor of *Life* Magazine, envisions a complete reversal of sex roles, in which the woman goes out to work each day, while "the more delicate male" sits home tending the fires and taking care of himself. But then he asks something that ought to give pause to the modern woman on her way to donning her first Brooks Brothers suit. About the submissive husband who is supposed to sit home and keep himself beautiful for the wife, Rosenfeld asks: "Ah, but will he? Or, while she's away at work . . . the icelady cometh . . . or the Fuller Brush lady?"

While the New Morality dims the behavioral differences between the two sexes, the New Biology is beginning to make it apparent that the physical differences, are not nearly as great as we thought, either. Dr. Peter Scott, writing in *New Scientist*, says, "The biologist is not particularly surprised that the line between male and female is not always as definitive as the signs on the respective toilet doors. . . ." After all, only that tiniest of all chromosomes, the Y, stands between men and what is rather inelegantly referred to as "femaleness." The male starts out life as something of a hermaphrodite and, even with that Y chromosome, is far from being home free; "he" could still become a little girl.

As Professor A. Jost put it at a Royal Society symposium on "The Determination of Sex" in 1969, "It's a struggle becoming a male. At several stages in his development, the little male embryo is in severe danger of becoming a female." About a week after the embryo attaches itself to the lining of the womb, the sex glands begin forming; at this point they are called the "indifferent gonads" because they are not yet exclusively male or female. Each gonad consists of two layers of tissue, which, together, assume the shape of an egg. The inner layer makes up the testis while the outer layer makes up the ovary. At about the fourth or fifth week of fetal life, one of two things happens. If the Y chromosome is present, a "male-induction factor" is released, presumably on command from genes in the Y chromosome, and this "dissolves" the outer, ovarian layer of the gonad, leaving only the testis. Or, if the Y chromosome is absent, nothing is released, and the outer layer just naturally prevails and produces an ovary. Hence, as Dr. Jost noted, it does take an extra effort to make a male. This is true again, later in fetal development, when the male sex hormone must intervene to keep the female sex ducts (present in all embryos, whether there is a Y chromosome or not) from asserting themselves, as they will do in the absence of any interference, and to keep the penis and scrotum from "degenerating" into the labia and clitoris of the female.

The "natural" tendency is always toward femaleness, and even when the Y chromosome is present, a breakdown in the male-induction chemistry can yield curious man-woman combinations. "Intersexuality," scientifically identified in humans only recently, can have varied results, such as the unfortunate "cock" that laid the egg. Among human intersexual conditions are "testicular feminization," in which an XY male is born with a vagina, normal female breasts, an infantile uterus, and testes that are sometimes embedded in the abdomen; female "pseudo (false) hermaphroditism," in which a woman comes equipped with ovaries but is otherwise masculinized; "true hermaphroditism," in which external genitals can appear to be all-male or all-female, even though both ovarian and testicular tissue (and very often both Fallopian tubes and male sex ducts) are present internally.

By now it should be obvious that sex is not quite as cut and dried as many of us would like to believe. In fact, science now insists that there are at least six different criteria that must be considered in what used to seem the very simple matter of identifying gender. These six "identity units," as they are called, are the external genitals, the internal gonads (ovaries or testes), the type of sex chromosomes (XX, XY, or a number of other combinations that have turned up, such as XYY, XXY, and even XXXXY), the characteristic hormones, the

assigned sex (what your parents thought you were), the
gender role (what you do), and what *you* think you are.
Surprisingly, the most important of these (the one that
can overrule all others in determining male or female
behavior, dress, and so on) is not the external genitals
but the assigned sex. Learning and experience, as Dr.
Scott notes, are more important than instinct or physiology in determining sexual attitudes and behavior. "If
the culture requires a man to eliminate all evidence of
bisexuality," he writes, "then that pattern must be
learned."

Where does all of this leave us? Well, we have seen
that our sexuality is not a rigid, either-or sort of thing;
it is highly susceptible (or vulnerable, again depending
on your feelings about the subject) to both sociological
and biological manipulation. Because man understands
this for the first time—and has the means of manipulation at hand for the first time—we may be in for some
radical changes. If we are choosing sex today, we may be
changing it tomorrow, through sophisticated genetic and
chemical engineering.

Chemical engineering has already done duty in the
field of sexual transformation. Because the fetus is so
malleable, so easily encouraged to disregard its genetic
sex, some scientists wondered whether a simple injection
of hormones or hormone suppressants during fetal development might not result in sexual change. Though
this has not yet been tried on the human fetus, one can

get a good idea of its effects by looking at some recent animal experiments.

Scientists working at the Schering Co. in Berlin injected into pregnant rats a chemical that neutralizes the male sex hormone. Male offspring were born with vaginas and, after being castrated and implanted with ovaries, became functioning females, capable of reproduction. The famed French biologist Jean Rostand reported that in other animal experiments, chemicals injected during the very earliest stages of embryonic development resulted in *complete* sexual reversals: embryos originally destined to be females turned out at birth to be perfect males and vice versa.

"Using salamanders and toads," Rostand said, "false females [meaning that they were genetic males transformed by hormones] have been coupled with true males and false males with true females, and from these unions descendants have been obtained that were the issue of two fathers or two mothers." These "homosexual unions," as Dr. Rostand called them, resulted in only male offspring when male parents were involved, and in female offspring in the other instance.

Genetic engineering (manipulation of the chromosomes and of the genes and nucleic acids that make up the chromosomes) could conceivably be used in the distant future to create a whole new breed of man—man capable of changing sex after birth and changing it repeatedly. We have already seen this sort of engineering at work in the cloning of plants and animals. Dr.

Rostand describes other experiments in which the genetic material can be manipulated in such a way that animals can be induced to reproduce by parthenogenesis (without male fertilization).

"It is now a regular thing," he noted, "for perfectly constituted living creatures to be born from a virgin egg without any help from a male, on condition that within the egg there has been produced a doubling of the chromosomes." Women, he predicted, may one day indulge regularly in this sort of "auto-adultery." Egg cells can be tricked into doubling themselves, usually by jolting them with chemicals; even pricking them with a pin can sometimes set them off. Dr. Rostand points to a number of variations on parthenogenesis that have been achieved in the laboratory, resulting in creatures that he describes as being of "somewhat baroque composition." A doubling of maternal chromosomes, for example, has been induced in *fertilized* eggs, resulting in offspring that, in Dr. Rostand's words, "must be considered their mother's children twice over and their father's only once."

These experiments are crude compared to what the genetic engineers hope to accomplish in years to come. When genetic "surgeons" are able to add, delete, and modify genes at will, man will be able to appropriate for himself a great number of biological capabilities that he presently lacks. As man moves out into new frontiers (the world beneath the sea and outer space), he may find it necessary and economical to change himself in a variety of ways. Perhaps he will want to assume the ability to breathe underwater with gills like fish and communicate by sonar—like porpoises. Or, like bees, he may find it helpful to extend his vision to parts of the spectrum presently invisible to the human eye or extend his hearing to ranges presently beyond his reach. On long space journeys, he may want to be genetically engineered to be able to hibernate like the hedgehog or regenerate damaged limbs and organs like the newt.

As for sex, we have only to look around us to get some grasp of the incredible possibilities. The animal kingdom is full of creatures whose sexual adaptability far outstrips our own. Take the slipper limpet, for example, a form of marine life common in the Atlantic Ocean. It starts out life without any sex whatever, grows into a male, and then into a hermaphrodite (possessing both male and female sex organs), before finally ending life as a female. The most interesting thing about the slipper limpet is its tendency to remain male as long as there is an adequate supply of females in the vicinity. It is only when there is a shortage of females that it will make the sacrifice and become a female. Other creatures, particularly of the annelid variety, exhibit an ability to change sex repeatedly, in order to change with conditions around them.

"Even in such advanced creatures as the bony fish," Dr. Scott writes in *New Scientist*, "some individuals of some species can function as females while they are young and as males later on, while others are normally hermaphroditic and may even fertilize their own eggs. Different species also show an expedient ability to advance or retard the onset of sexual maturity, so that some are born with mature testes and may mate within two days of birth. Eels may delay their sexual maturation for years. . . . The lot of the male is not always enviable. In one case, *Ceratius*, the male is absorbed into his wife's body until nothing remains of him but the sex organs. He has no senses, no alimentary canal, no independent movement—the ultimate in subjugation."

Unless all the genetic surgeons of the future are female, it is not likely that man will pattern himself after *Ceratius*. But it is not inconceivable that man will want to emulate some of these other creatures. It has frequently been said that if men could be women and women men—even for a few minutes—many of the conflicts that have simmered between the two sexes these many centuries might fade away overnight. At any rate, it is indisputable that the sort of "sexual dimorphism" under discussion here would provide life with a whole new dimension—one that might prove highly practical in the event of wars or other catastrophes that decimate one sex or the other, in the new frontiers of outer space, and in other situations in which people are isolated from members of the opposite sex.

In the world of the future, parents may no longer worry about whether their next child will be a boy or a girl: he may be *both!*

Index

DAVID M. RORVIK is a graduate of the University of Montana and holds a Master of Science degree from the Columbia Graduate School of Journalism in New York. Following a Pulitzer Traveling Fellowship to Africa in 1967, Mr. Rorvik worked two years for *Time* as a Medicine and Science reporter. Now a free-lance writer, his articles appear frequently in such national magazines as *Look, Esquire, Science Digest, McCall's,* and *Playboy.*

LANDRUM B. SHETTLES, M.D., Ph.D. is Associate Professor of Obstetrics and Gynecology at Columbia University's College of Physicians and Surgeons, and an attending physician at Columbia-Presbyterian Medical Center, New York City. Dr. Shettles, who received his M.D. and Ph.D. degrees from The Johns Hopkins University, is internationally known for the discovery and identification of male and female producing sperms. A frequent contributor to distinguished professional journals, Dr. Shettles is a member of numerous medical societies, including the World Medical Association, the American College of Obstetricians and Gynecologists, and the (British) Royal Society of Health.